...AND
WE WILL
BECOME
A HAPPY
ENDING

027/100

...AND WE WILL BECOME A HAPPY ENDING

Joe Manafo, on behalf of theStory

Published & Designed by: Storyboard Solutions Inc., Sarnia, ON.
Edited by: Bren Melles
Sound Advice: Sarah Manafo

www.thestory.ca

CONTENTS

DISCLAIMER

While God is spirit---neither masculine nor feminine---the English language is restrictive and makes us choose gender specific pronouns. We've chosen to use He and His, not because God is male (because God is not), but because English words fail us when we speak of God.

INTRODUCTION
Start with the ending.

Inevitably, we must begin with the ending. Our present is informed by our future, our today makes better sense when we understand our tomorrow.

If that feels as if things are out of order, it's because they are. But not for long.

This book is made up of three movements. We start with the end in mind (The Happy Ending), a final picture that influences who we are in the present. Near the middle we uncover glimpses of who is behind that final picture (The Author) and use common words and images to try and make sense of how it all comes together. The last pages of this book are a brief description of our greatest present challenges (Out of Order) and how we might participate in reclaiming what has long been lost.

Each thought in this book has been limited to a one page small burst of words with the hope that it would not be so conclusive as to close the canon, but instead act as a good starting point for an even better conversation.

The stories and sayings, ponderings and pictures in this book capture the hope of a very small group of people who intend on re-ordering what is out of order---starting with themselves. That's essentially what this book is about: why theStory is the way it is and why we give a damn.

Many voices are woven into this project---some credited, some not. It's hard to remember where one voice ends and the others begin, or at what moment another's experience changed our understanding. To those we've rendered unintentionally anonymous, we ask for your aggressive forgiveness.

We borrowed the name of the book from a song called "Chariot" by a band named Page France. Punch "Page France Chariot on New Year's Eve" into YouTube and you'll witness more than a basement concert. It is a call to worship, a reminder, and a hope. And yes, we realize that while some of you may have heard the slang term 'happy ending' in the context of a conversation about a massage parlour, in the spirit of this book, we'd be remiss if we didn't reverse, redeem, and reorder that image into something new.

Lastly, we love Sarnia, Ontario and specifically the people and neighbourhoods that make up our waterfront downtown. This book was written with you in mind and is dedicated to you. You are beloved.

Joe Manafo
Summer 2012

"If there is no point in the story as a whole, there is no point in my own action. If the story is meaningless, any action of mine is meaningless...so the answer to the question 'Who am I?' can only be given if we ask 'What is my story?' and that can only be answered if there is an answer to the further question, 'What is the whole story of which my story is a part?'"

-Lesslie Newbigin

THE HAPPY ENDING

How the church is the pilot project for how things will ultimately be.

Postcards from exotic locations always seem to find their way to our fridge doors. The perfect postcard photo is always accompanied by a personal note---"Weather is great! Wish you were here! See you soon!" It's a snapshot of another place and time, and an invitation to join our friends in their experience.

The Happy Ending is the perfect snapshot of God's perfect intention for all creatures and creation. It's the way things are going to one day look.

The Happy Ending is the personal note, the witness that says we are living proof that Jesus has not given up on this world.

The Happy Ending is the invitation to be fully human, the link between heaven and earth, soil and spirit.

The church is God's pilot project for The Happy Ending. Expressed in love, the church is a collection of imperfect people who - despite their differences and preferences - recognize that there is a better way to live with each other, with the earth, and in relation to God. Call it a practice session or a dry run, the church is sorting out what it will be like to live as we were always intended to live. Think of it as a jumpstart on The Happy Ending.

Rooted Encaustic Icon by Natalie Salminen Rude. Original hangs at 179 Christina St. N, Sarnia. Prints of Rooted/Tabled/Risked hang in the dwellings of families who call theStory home.

We live in a world of competing narratives. The dominant stories of our time are based on a string of lies, each one covering up the last in an effort to obscure the trail. Time passes, the weeds thicken, memories grow cold, and we are left dull and dazed. People stop thinking and loving, making the lies all the more believable. Chalk one up for evil.

But we are storytellers of a different kind. We tell an alternative tale, one rooted in all things good and very good (Genesis 1:31). In turn, we allow good to take root in us. Eventually it blooms from within, inoculating, transforming, regenerating. Next, it goes to seed and becomes contagious (Mark 4:26-28; Mark 4:30-32) establishing outposts of truth tellers in places both feared and forgotten. Chalk two up for good.

As good takes root in and around us, lies are exposed and all evil begins to unravel.

We become a Happy Ending when we find ourselves rooted in the greater Story.

"Our lives must find their place in a greater story or they will find their place in a lesser story."
-H. Stephen Shoemaker

"It is not enough that we announce the good news, explain it or whip up enthusiasm for it. It must be lived---lived in detail, lived in the streets and on the job, lived in the bedrooms and kitchens, lived through cancer and divorce, lived with children and marriage." -Eugene Peterson

Tabled Encaustic Icon by Natalie Salminen Rude.

"This is our vocation: to convert the enemy into a guest and to create the free and fearless space where brotherhood and sisterhood can be formed and fully experienced." -Henri Nouwen

Jesus sat at all the wrong tables with all the wrong people. Food, drink, drunks, whores, and hospitality. It is to this very table that he invites us to sit. It's an "All you can Seat!" affair, with no reservations required. Spots are limited only by the number of guests that choose to attend.

The table is a place of unending first starts. (Matthew 18:21-23)

The table is a place where doubt is validated and questions carry no penalty. (John 20:26-28)

The table is a place where the divide between the sacred and secular dissolves. (1 Corinthians 8:1-7)

The table is the place where our deepest wounds are healed. (1 Peter 2:23-25)

To this end, Jesus commissions his followers to be party planners. To recreate his table in homes and whore houses alike. To invite any and all, to serve well and plenty, until each has their fill and all the leftovers are collected (John 6:1-14).

We become a Happy Ending when we sit with those whom Jesus sat, and are referred to as Jesus was, "drinking and eating, a glutton and a drunkard, a friend of tax collectors and sinners." (Luke 7:34)

"The place to which God calls you is where your deep gladness and the world's deep hunger meet." -Frederick Buechner

"In celebrating their fellowship around the table, the early Christians testified that the messianic age, often pictured as a banquet, had begun." -John Howard Yoder

Risked Encaustic Icon by Natalie Salminen Rude.

"When the forms of an old culture are dying, a new culture is created by a few people who are not afraid to be insecure." -Rudolf Bahro

We can't afford to risk because we have too much to lose. (Luke 18:18-29) Bred on money-back guarantees, pre-emptive strikes, airbags and fortune cookies, we've fabricated an illusion of safety that leaves us with more fear than security. Adding insult to injury, this same fear leaks into our souls, locking us up to the point that instead of embracing risk as the most basic building block of faith, we create a buffer of systems and institutions that keep trouble tidy and controlled, and us at a safe distance.

Jesus calls us to embrace a holy-insecurity---to push all our chips to the middle of the table and take a chance on the notion that what he said is actually true (John 16:33). In direct contrast to all our inherited superstitions, we now understand that in order to be first, we have to be last; in order gain, we have to lose; in order to live, we have to die. (Luke 9:23-25; Matthew 19:29,30; Mark 9:33-35) We intentionally choose downward mobility in an upwardly mobile culture.

We become a Happy Ending when we find security in the embrace of risk.

"When the story of these times gets written, we want it to say that we did all we could, and it was more than anyone could have imagined." -Bono

"To live meaningfully is to be in perpetual risk." -Robert McKhee

"Defiant Imagination" installation from the Tabled.ca collection.

IMAGINATION

"If you don't use your own imagination, somebody else is going to use it for you." -Ron Sukenick

"What has captured our imagination? When was the last time you saw a movie on peace?"
  -Stanley Hauwerwas

"Imagination is more important than knowledge." -Albert Einstein

"Imagination rules the world." -Napoleon Bonaparte

"We have to help people see that when the local congregation meets, we are engaged in an act of alternative imagination." -Walter Brueggemann

Faith is an art, not a science. At its best, organized religion is like a well ventilated art room stocked with paints, easels and drop cloths. It's humankind's best effort at creating an environment where imagination comes to life over and over again.

This kind of imagination unmasks and unpacks systems that oppress and devalue. It subverts evil and leads to superior alternatives. It grants us permission to ask all the hard questions without fear or penalty. It gives us insight into our world and the worlds beyond us. In turn, it frees us from the incarceration of greed and inequality where we've become dangerously comfortable.

Without fail, the underpinnings of every society and culture eventually make themselves known through the imaginations and memories of its people.

Where are our best memories found?

What are our dominant metaphors?

What are we dreaming about?

"Dreams, by definition, are supposed to be unique and imaginative. Yet the bulk of the population is dreaming the same dream. It's a dream of wealth, power, fame, plenty of sex and exciting recreational opportunities. What does it mean when a whole culture dreams the same dreams?" -Kalle Lasn

We become a Happy Ending when our imaginations are untangled, and our lives, friendships and neighbourhoods are a living gallery of art---the masterpieces they were always intended to be.

"Dropped" multi-site art installation exploring grounded ideas from above. First Friday, Downtown Sarnia, September 2012.

"The world is not a film which can be re-run; it is a single impromptu performance, a piece of street theater by a pickup company who never saw each other before or since, who did what they did, tossed off whatever lines came into their heads, barged into each other, punched each other, kicked and bit, or kissed and made-up as it seemed convenient at the time---and closed to rave reviews with a rousing improvisation of the New Jerusalem that made everyone go shivery all over." -Robert Capon

In the 1991 film "What About Bob?," Bill Murray plays the part of an obsessive compulsive psychiatric patient who is the ultimate undoing of his therapist. After the release of the film, it was noted that an accurate script could not be written until after the film had been completed. The reason? In moments of creative brilliance, Murray improvised his way through many of the scenes. He was able to depart from the original script while keeping with the original storyline.

Humans must live in this same tension.

"The task is not so much a matter of being able to quote the earlier script as it is to be able to continue it, to imaginatively discern what shape this story now must take in our changing cultural context." -N.T. Wright

In times that are less than ideal, Christians are called toward an improvisational ethic. Fully present in our current scene yet fully aware of the final act, we are summoned to negotiate hope and despair, brokenness and healing in such a way that we bring heaven to earth---that is, we work hand in hand with God for the restoration of all things.

We know the story. We know our part in it. Without rehearsal, we live out our scenes redeeming and renewing, setting wrongs to rights. And when others join us by acting in the same way, aware of the story and the parts, we call them the church. Thus, by way of improvisation, the church becomes God's Pilot Project for the New Jerusalem. [Revelation 21:1-5] It's the campaign for real humanity*, the way things were always meant to be, and one day, fully will be.

We become a Happy Ending when we improv our way from evil to good, when we play the hand we've been dealt the best way that it can be played. And, in the end, each of us is invited to the cast party.

"This great drama is a great play in search of actors, and there are parts for everyone, you and me included."
-N.T. Wright

*Wording borrowed from Rowan Williams

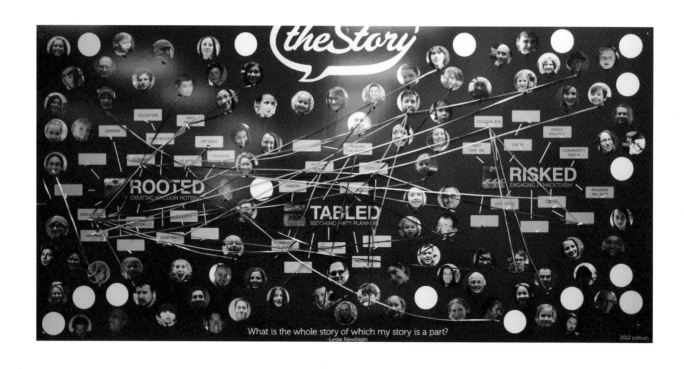

theStory Family Tree. Connecting the who, what and why on our shift as a local church.

"It's not the long walk home that will change this heart, but the welcome I receive with every start."
-Mumford & Sons

"We live in an atmosphere choked with the fumes of un-grace. Grace comes from the outside, as a gift and not an achievement. How easily it vanishes from our dog-eat-dog, survival-of-the-fittest, look-out-for-number-one-world." -Philip Yancey

It seems painfully obvious that God has checked out. When one starts to add up the stories of betrayal, conflict, injustice and pain, divine abandonment appears to be the logical explanation. On trial for neglect and destructive disregard for life, God now becomes responsible for all evil. And God is.

God assumes responsibility by personifying grace. Grace isn't afraid to get dirty. Grace has calloused hands. Grace fills the gap when ends can't meet. (Luke 18:1-8) Grace rolls out of bed late at night to help [Luke 11:5-8], but then shows up on time for work the next morning. Grace wears a blue collar.

Grace is one of the ways we recognize God's active presence in our world. If God is guilty of anything it is that God values human freedom so much that we are allowed to do as we please. And if it seems like we never see God, it is likely because God works nights on the janitorial shift, cleaning up after yesterday and ensuring that mercy will be fresh and new tomorrow. (Lamentations 3:22-23)

We become a Happy Ending when we button up the blue collar of grace, when we respect the freedom of others while remaining active and on call in extending mercy.

"The time you need grace most is when you deserve it least." -Katie Morris

"Have courage for the great sorrows of life and patience for the small ones; and when you have laboriously accomplished your daily task, go to sleep in peace. God is awake." -Victor Hugo

"Our Apologies" Reverse Confessional. First Friday, Downtown Sarnia, January 2010.

"Not forgiving is like drinking rat poison and then waiting for the rat to die." -Anne Lamott

Forgiveness is the new language for the new world. We freely forgive because we remember that we've been freely forgiven. (Colossians 2:13-15) Often we feel that if we keep record of the wrongs done to us, we hold some sort of power over the offender. Nothing could be further from the truth. When we hold onto anger and un-forgiveness, we hold it over our own heads. We fool ourselves into thinking that we're somehow getting even when all we're really doing is sequestering ourselves behind bars of fear.

"To forgive is to set a prisoner free and discover that the prisoner was you." -Lewis B. Smedes

Free from having to keep track of others' wrongs, and forever carrying a heavy list of transgressions, we now have the capacity---and the disposition---to carry the trouble of others. Jesus calls us to join him in the middle of the mess, not to distance ourselves from it. (Matthew 25:31-46)

"The cross says the pain stops here. The way of the cross is a way of absorbing pain, not passing it on." -Parker Palmer

"The powers of evil are defeated not by some overwhelming display of divine power but by the weakness of Christ's death." -Andrew Lincoln

We become a Happy Ending when remember that we've been forgiven and do likewise. As we free others, we free ourselves.

"Expecting." Advent 2009
teaching series art.

HAPPY ARE THE WRITE-OFFS

Happy are the murderers and child molesters
Happy are the brutal and the bigoted
Happy are the drug lords and pornographers
Happy are the criminals, the terrorists the perverted the filthy, and the filthy rich
Happy is rapist Paul Bernardo
Happy is the Taliban
Happy is North Korea's criminally insane Kim Jong-Il
Happy is BP and its oil stained hands
(Matthew 5:3-10 in modern language and context; partly inspired and borrowed from Dallas Willard)

Jesus' words feel counterintuitive---but maybe that was the point. In an attempt to rearrange the mental building blocks that make up our understanding of God's identity and intentions, our sensibilities are confronted by the breadth of God's forgiveness.

Good news for all is the order of the hour. We are all happy not because of our brokenness, but because God's reach is not too short to rescue us. Every last one of us. Even the worst of us. Even those who've yet to realize that sin lumps us all into one undeniable category.

"The relationship between the obedience of God's people and triumph of God's cause is not a relationship between cause and effect but one of cross and resurrection." -John Howard Yoder

"The sermon on the mount, therefore, is not a list of requirements, but rather a description of the life of a people gathered by and around Jesus. To be saved is to be so gathered." -Stanley Hauerwaus

We become a Happy Ending when we enter into God's good news---we are both redeemed and can be reborn.

Shalynn Silvestri's baptism. Lake Huron, July 2008.

HOLY WHOLENESS!

"Holiness, Jesus saw, was not something to be protected; rather it was God's miraculous power of transformation. God's holiness cannot be soiled; rather, it is a cleansing and healing agent. It does not need to be shut up and quarantined in the temple; it is now, through Jesus' healings and fellowship with the despised and rejected, breaking out into the world to transform it." -Walter Wink

"There is a holiness sometimes in keeping it together." -Sarah Masen

"So remember, you who profess to be followers of the Lord Jesus, that to you indifference is impossible! You must bless the church and the world by your holiness, or you will curse them both by your hypocrisy and inconsistency. In the visible church it is most true that 'no man liveth unto himself, and no man dieth unto himself.'" -Charles Spurgeon

Holiness isn't sinning less, it's loving more.* Our morals have nothing to do with either our salvation or our damnation. We are forgiven and redeemed only because God accepts us in whatever state we find ourselves. And we are damned only if we stupidly (neither faithfully nor wisely) insist on rejecting that acceptance by unbelief. (Matthew 24:45-51)

In this light, holiness looks less like personal health insurance and more like universal health care. It shifts from keeping the peace to mischief that uncorks the peace. It morphs from thoughtless routine to regular interruptions that reveal our true purpose.

Holiness is the change agent by which we are made whole. We are healed as we extend healing. We are set apart from our false selves and for the better way.

"I believe there is a Creator, a revolutionary force at work that is compelling us towards love, peace, health, and wholeness. In recognizing such a presence we must begin to care for creation, for humanity and for the sparks of divinity in every aspect of life. We must accept the invitation to work with God in his redeeming story, Jesus' story, our story, The Story." -John Howard Yoder

We become a Happy Ending when God's holiness infuses us and transforms us, making us whole.

*Wording borrowed from David Fitch

The O'Darling performing at theStory for the Empty Spaces concert series, November 2009.

Sarnia Urban Sports, dodgeball, June 2008.

EXCLUSIVELY INCLUSIVE

"By necessity, the knowledge of God is always partial." -Jean Vanier

"Christianity comes about when someone does something. It is a way to be witnessed, not a proposition to be proven." -John Caputo

"The essence of other religions is advice. Christianity is essentially news." -Tim Keller

We are curators of the most important announcement on earth. By it we see all of life differently and a new way of being becomes second nature. We are at our best when we are radically abandoned to its telling and retelling. Though our natural default is to compare answers, weigh facts and organize distinctions, the announcement of all of things being made new trumps all categories and opinions. (2 Corinthians 5)

The good news is exclusively inclusive (Luke 14:15-24; Galatians 3:26-29). Within its reach there is room for disagreement, preference, questions of any kind, and doubt. Each of us is included in God's greater intentions until we decide to opt out.

This makes for some awkward discomfort, for we're in the nasty habit of making enemies of those we don't understand or agree with.

"Muslims, homosexuals, and abortion doctors are not the enemy.
Hitler and Obama, Liberals and Conservatives are not the enemy.
The thing inside of us that tells us to hate these people, ironically enough, is the enemy." -Mike Gary Cole

This is not to say that the world isn't filled with both good and evil or truth and lies. What it does elude to, however, is that God is less concerned about our position on issues and more concerned about disposition towards others. (Philippians 2:1-11)

"Spiritual formation is the great reversal: from being the subject who controls all other things to being a person who is shaped by the presence, purpose and power of God in all things." -Ross Mulholland

It is in the Christian DNA to gather in the outcast, the ones that are unlovable, to uphold the cause of the oppressed, and to love our enemies (Matthew 5:44, Psalm 146:7; James 1:27). This is the announcement of God's good news. This is how God's transformative work seeps into our bones. This is a renovation of the heart. But be careful – it's highly contagious.

We become a Happy Ending when we trust and allow God to do his promised transformative work in each one of us.

"The Values Experiment." . First Friday, Downtown Sarnia, March 2010.

"Christian faith at rock bottom conflicts with North American culture, even subverts it…the practicing Christian should look like a Martian. He or she will never feel at home in the commodity kingdom. If the Christian does feel at home, something is drastically wrong." -John F. Kavanaugh

"Shopping occupies a role in society that once belonged only to religion---the power to give meaning and construct identity." -Skye Jethani

"The Christian is an incessant revolutionary. He is always everywhere, in revolt---not for himself but for humanity." -William Stringfellow

Our humanity and the humanity of others are robbed when we treat each other like commodities. Relationships become transactions as people become products to be consumed. This exploitive way of being devalues us to the point where we become disposable.

"People, even more than things, have to be restored, renewed, reclaimed and redeemed. Never throw out anybody." -Audrey Hepburn

Our imaginations have been co-opted when we perpetuate the deadly patterns of human commodification. St. Paul reintroduces an old ethic to combat these tendencies when he writes:

"Put to death, therefore, whatever belongs to your earthly nature: sexual immorality, impurity, lust, evil desires and greed, which is idolatry. Because of these, the wrath of God is coming. You used to walk in these ways, in the life you once lived. But now you must also rid yourselves of all such things as these: anger, rage, malice, slander, and filthy language from your lips. Do not lie to each other, since you have taken off your old self with its practices and have put on the new self, which is being renewed in knowledge in the image of its Creator." (Collosians 3:5-10)

Kill it before it kills you. Do away with the vestiges that once had a stranglehold on your life. Abandon the false allegiances and pretentious sovereignties that have held you captive. You are better than this. Don't belittle yourself, living from one hit to the next in a loop of unending self-gratification and glorification.

"As long as I am plagued by doubts about my self-worth, I keep looking for gratification from people around me…But when I detach myself from this need for human affirmation and discover that it is with the Lord that I find my true self… pain inflicted by people will not touch me in the center." -Henri Nouwen

We become a Happy Ending when we cherish each other as we are cherished by the Creator.

"To return evil for good is devilish. To return good for good is human. To return good for evil is divine."

-Alfred Plummer

THE AUTHOR
By Whom the Happy Ending is possible.

We live in an "in-between" time. The past behind us, the future in front of us as we straddle the gap between how things are and how things are meant to be. It's a cosmic case of middle child syndrome. We're familiar with the beginning and aware of the end, but somehow feel uncomfortable and even at times ignored in what we know as our present.

It can be dark living in the shadows of seemingly more important people and epochs. So dark that we question the Author and demand that He take responsibility for the world we've inherited. And, to our surprise, He agrees, and assumes both responsibility and remedy. Evil is His problem and He knows it. And for those of us with more questions than answers, this realization begins to put us at ease because the path to The Happy Ending is lit by the Light Himself.

C.S. Lewis once said that what the church needs isn't better arguments, but better metaphors. In this section we've cobbled together some real-time metaphors for God. This isn't an exhaustive list but a thrift store collection of images that give credence to God's activity in this middle time. By God, The Happy Ending is possible.

Interpretd by Ryan Young

GOD IS A GAMBLER

He is all in on every hand we play—win or lose, good or evil.
He risks all for the sake of our freedom.

GOD IS A CROOK

And He dies like a crook to prove it.
He steals the sin that is ours and refuses to
reveal its whereabouts lest we attempt to reclaim it.

GOD IS A CO-SIGNER

He bears the responsibility of the inevitable default on our payment and promises.
(And the bank knows he's good for it)

GOD IS AN ALARM CLOCK

Jesus spent his three days of death waking those who had fallen asleep to the new day of his reign.
The snooze bar of sin disabled, the alarm has been going off ever since. [Eph 5:13-15]

if you forgive people enough, you belong to them, and they to you

Interpreted by Troy Shantz

GOD IS A SQUATTER

He inhabits conflict and makes the all the disasters
of our histories the sacraments of His saving presence.

GOD IS A CENTERFOLD

At the incarnation He is exposed, adored and violated.
The money shot: Cross not crotch, where blood bests semen.

GOD IS AN IRON WORKER

He bids us to "beat our swords into plowshares and our spears into pruning hooks".
Warriors into gardeners is His aim.

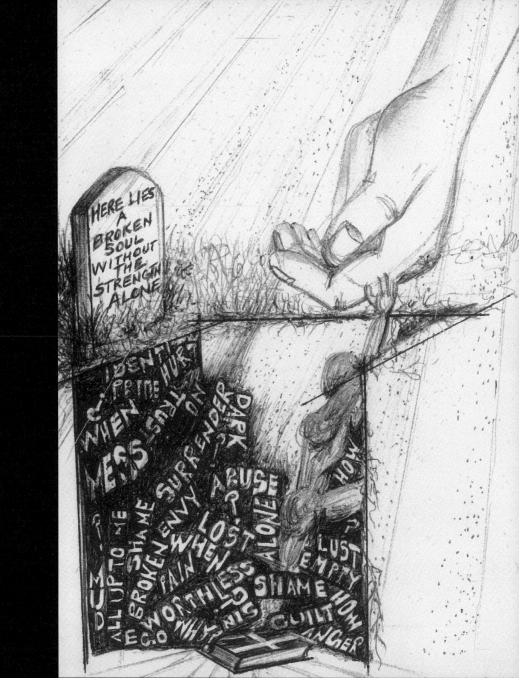

GOD IS A BODY SNATCHER

Looting the graves of the living, God unearths our true humanity and buries Himself in our place.
Funeral industry beware.

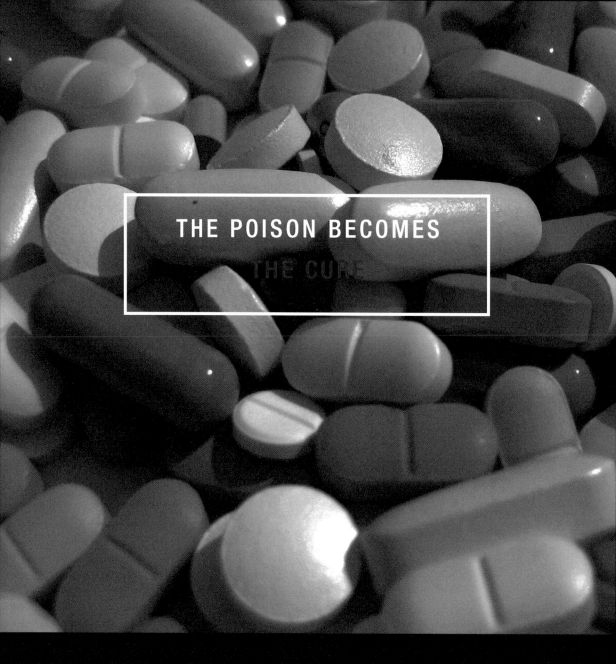

THE POISON BECOMES
THE CURE

Interpreted by Elizabeth Cowie

GOD IS A SELF-EXPERIMENTER

The great physician infects himself with the Poison to become the Cure.
Evil is taken out as it is taken in.

Interpreted by
Carolyn Amorin

GOD IS A DEALER

Pushing hope at the intersections of our souls and our neighbourhoods,
He reclaims lost territory from the death dealers and legalizes peace.

Interpreted by Natalie Rude

GOD IS A DJ

Mashing our original tunes one into the next, He spins a new song.
Tempos and tirades, styles and sleaze are of no challenge.
The base track of His redemption unites them all.

god is left handed

Interpreted
by Marty
Oblak

GOD IS LEFT HANDED

Tying His right hand [power via military, political, economical might] behind his back,
He uses His left [subtle, hidden, paradoxical power] hand to bring about good—for everyone.

Interpreted by Jared Robinson

GOD IS A FASHION DESIGNER

He invites us to clothe ourselves with His best pieces:
Compassion, Kindness, Humility, Gentleness, Peace and Forgiveness. [Phil. 4].
The world is His catwalk, we are His models.

GOD IS A STAGEHAND

He works behind the curtains setting up the scenery, lights, sounds, props and special effects.
Vital yet often overlooked, He is at his best when unnoticed.
He is at the service of the story and His joy is found with the actors regardless of their performance.

GOD IS A CLOSE TALKER

He is most often heard in whispers causing us to lean in and draw close.
While some have taken to yell on His behalf, it has only caused others to cover their ears. [1 Kings 19]
Silence becomes a rite as we become deaf to competing voices.

GOD IS A LAND LADY

She owns the building we live in and is responsible for repairs and property maintenance. [Psalm 24; Revelation 21] As Her long term leasers, it is in our contract to keep it clean and safe, that is, to live in unity with the soil, each other and the Land Lady. [Genesis 2]

GOD IS A MASTER OF DISGUISES

Recently He has been seen as a starved foreigner who lacks health care and is a felon—likely on charges of public nudity. [Matthew 25]. He will often camouflage himself amongst those we fear and hate most in an effort to help us sort out our own identities.

Interpreted by Nathan Colquhoun

GOD IS UNETHICAL

He lets liars, murderers and molesters off the hook and even those who feel their infractions are less detestable are allowed to go free. He insists that no one will get what they deserve. [Psalm 103; Matthew 5]

GOD IS A LIQUIDATOR

Less is divinely more as generosity begets generosity.
Gain through loss, life via death, pay it forward and backwards.
Grace undercuts entitlement and the tab is on the Lord's house.

GOD IS A CHEATER

He passed the winning card under the table of his death for all to see.
The game is fixed. So are we.

"We all have to decide how much sin we can live with."

-Nucky Thompson, Boardwalk Empire

OUT OF ORDER
The fix we find ourselves in & how evil is deathly contagious.

There's nothing quite like a fight to pull people together. From school yards to contested territories, superiority and innocence are claimed in the same breath by all parties. Villains and heroes are cast, blame is laid, sides are set, and scores are kept. Harmony is breached and death comes into our homes to roost. This is the blow by blow account of our race. Out of sync and step with the Creator and creation, it seems like the replacement parts to repair the damage we've done have long been out of production. Called out to be lovers and caregivers, we outsourced our identities to the lowest bidder: pride.

The results have been corrosive. We've adopted systems that perpetuate brokenness and have given full clearance for thieves to steal, kill and destroy. God's proper order has been tampered with, terms have been violated, and we are found so deep in dysfunction that fully untangling ourselves by our own means is no longer possible. The problem is nested inside each of us as we self-sabotage and become accomplices in our own demise. When we give into the temptation to look out for only ourselves, we intentionally vandalize peace. Cornelius Plantinga calls it "a culpable disturbance of shalom." We've often called it by another name: sin.

The way things are is not the way they were intended to be. Sin is the poison that keeps us from being healthy. Sin is the one-way ticket away from wholeness. Sin passes lies off as truth, commodifies beauty, regulates social classes, abuses freedoms, twists friendships, estranges family, and ultimately betrays us from being our true selves. It's the most corrupt of all pyramid schemes—everyone who plays loses.

Given the state of things, we must rightfully identify our antagonist. Too often, we've suspected people we disagree with or people groups who do not share our convictions as the enemy. Other times, we've blamed demons and devils as the root cause of our problems. But even in that line up of easy targets, none fit the description or match the police sketch. This only leaves us with one possible culprit: ourselves.

Sin—this out of order way of living—is personified when we allow it to get the better of us. Evil comes to life when we let it come to life. It's not even our default setting! At our very beginning, God described us as "very good" and to this day, by God's strength and Spirit, God continues to believe it to be true. Our worst enemy breeds inside of us and becomes contagious when we let it overtake our heart, soul, mind and strength. When we love ourselves above all else we're doomed. In this final section we'll take a snapshot of where we've been missing the point and articulate why we find ourselves in the mess that we're in. The Good News is that there is another way: The Happy Ending.

Front entrance at 179 Christina Street North

RHYTHMS

Can we live 24/6 in a 24/8 world?

"Above all, remember that the meaning of life is to live it as if it were a work of art. You're not a machine."
-Abraham Heschel

Life is a dance. An improvisational, unscripted work of art set to sound and tempo. When Creator and creation are in tune and in step, the display is magical. Love and hope, pain and grief are key changes taken in stride. All of life harmonizes in an ode to joy.

This is made possible only because art, at its best, is not measured by a score or a judge. Value cannot be attached because calculators don't go that high. And even if they could, adding the numbers would be a disappointing case of missing the point.

When the point gets missed, we get suckered into counterfeits and cheap imitations of true life: knock offs, a million sold, paint by numbers, copies of copies. This type of existence is a violent one. Immersed in a cult of speed, productivity, efficiency, gain and growth, insanity is touted as normal—or at the very least, strongly suggested. Is this really how we were meant to live?

Being in sync with God is less like adding and subtracting and more like humming a tune that's stuck in your head and allowing it to put a directional spring in your step. That spring leads us in the direction of sacred rhythms—rhythms of grace, awareness, surrender and peace. On God's dance mix there is no room for the rhythms of production (you're only as valuable as what you can do), the rhythms of speed and space (you must move at an insane clip in an effort to fill yourself with stuff), or rhythms of fear (you're not good enough, so what are you going to do about it?).

The conga line of true living is a long (and slow) obedience in the same direction that reminds us of who we are and Whose we are (Genesis 1:26-27; Zephaniah 3:17; Jonah 4:2; Psalm 103:11-13). It sharpens our ability to recognize Jesus in the midst of everyday life (John 21), and it purposefully propels us 'out there' for God's glory and for the benefit of humanity (Matthew 4:1-11).

God's dance card isn't full, and God invites us to invite others onto the dance floor.

We Re-Order the world when we are in sync and in rhythm to the tune of redemption.

"Normal is getting dressed in clothes that you buy for work and driving through traffic in a car that you are still paying for—in order to get to the job you need to pay for the clothes and the car, and the house you leave vacant all day so you can afford to live in it." -Ellen Goodman

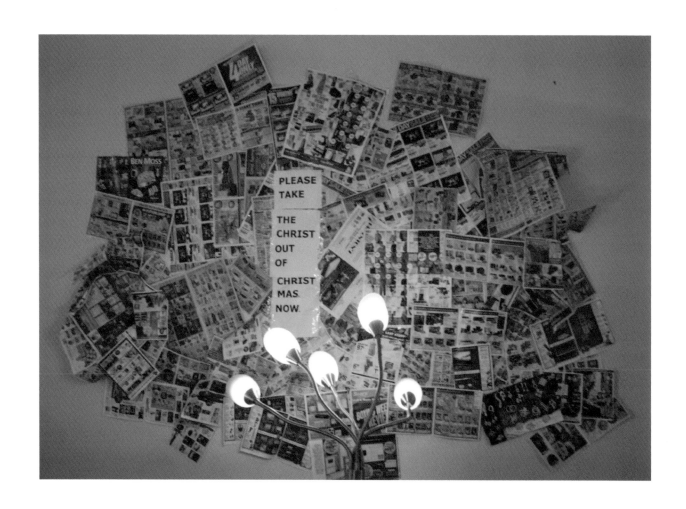

Worship station, Christmas 2007

UNCOMMON CENTS

"The opposite of poverty is not wealth. The opposite of both poverty and wealth is community."
-Jürgen Moltmann

The things we own end up owning us. We're at the mercy of debts that rise, values that plummet and markets that misbehave. Richard Foster cuts to the chase by saying, "Covetousness we call ambition. Hoarding we call prudence. Greed we call industry." Obsessed with wants and must haves we are at odds with ourselves. Working to live has quietly turned into living to work. We hate it, but can't get enough of it.

Like designer drugs it's become chic to lose control. (Luke 12:16-21)
Like a gated community, what was designed to keep people out now locks people in. (Luke 16:19-31)

But what if self-worth and net worth are not the same thing? (Rick Warren)
But what if the material needs of my neighbor are my spiritual needs? (Lithuanian rabbi Israel Salanter)

In many native American cultures, the "potlatch" or giveaway was at the heart of their economic system. One gathered wealth, not to accumulate for oneself, but to give it away and invest it in the community. The richest person in the community is the one who gives the most away. (Leonard Sweet)

The privilege is all ours:

To hold people tightly and possessions loosely. (Mark 10:17-27)
To spend ourselves on things of true value that have no have shelf life. (Matthew 6:19-21)

The joke has finally run its course. No longer can a 20% of the world be worried about slimming down, while 80% are concerned with hunger. One in two children are living in poverty. Our world is in the red. (World Bank stats as of 2012)

He who dies with the most toys is not the winner, but the biggest disappointment.

We Re-Order the world when we steward our gifts and resources for the benefit of others.

"If I have it, and somebody else needs it, it's theirs." -Cornel West

"The way of the [Christian] is not the way of upward mobility in which our world has invested so much but the way of downward mobility ending at the cross. This might sound morbid and masochistic, but for those who have heard the voice of the first love and said yes to it, the downward-moving way of Jesus is the way to the joy and the peace of God, a joy and peace that is not of this world." -Henri Nouwen

SOUNDTRACKS

April 2010 | thestory.ca | 519.381.6998 | 179 Christina St N | 24/7 and intentionally on Sundays

"Soundtracks" teaching series art

"Good communities are spaces where people love one another enough that they're not afraid of disagreements." -Stanley Hauerwas

We all have a Soundtrack tied to our existence. Over and over the sounds of preference, understanding, and desire play out in our heads and in our actions. Often, we're happy to express and share in each other's Soundtracks—until, that is, someone else's song selection clashes with ours. At that point, things get awkward and the music either goes mute or gets cranked to 11.

There is a Soundtrack linked to our sexuality and relationships. In our time it feels like the loudest of all anthems as we've lifted sex to the greatest of human experiences. Sought after and chased, we are more than willing to give up anything and everything for it as if it was the pinnacle of our identity. Add in the same-sex ballad to the top 40 and we have a defining moment for the 21st century local church.

We must do away with the stale songs of fear, prejudice and stereotype and sing again the old standards of hope, grace and love.

Our greatest challenge is not "What are we going to do about gays?" but "How must we treat and engage people regardless of sexuality, disagreement, offence or hurt?"

We must intentionally move away from dividing and distancing ourselves from individuals and groups, and towards living in the tension of conviction, unanswered questions and peace. This movement is fueled by a limitless supply of grace for all (regardless of sexual orientation or behaviour) and a ferocious disdain for sin (again understanding that sin is an anti-reaction to God's order and intent which inevitably leads to ruin).

Our posture must be welcoming. (Matthew 18:4-6; Romans 3:21-24)
Our disposition, transformative. (2 Corinthians 3:18)

Choosing to ignore the different sounds won't make them go away. So instead, the ideal option as followers of Jesus is to listen well.

We Re-Order the world when the soundtrack of prejudice and pride is drowned out by the melodies of grace and love.

"Our task is not to lock into an ethic that has been frozen in time, but to pursue an ultimate ethic, one reflected in the redemptive spirit of Scripture. As a community born into the twenty first century, we must not be limited to a mere enactment of the text's isolated words. It is our sacred calling to champion its spirit." -William J. Webb

"Intersections" installation from the Tabled.ca collection

INTERSECTIONS

"Worlds are colliding Jerry!" -George Costanza, Seinfeld

Worlds are colliding—heaven and earth; hell and earth. Daily. Each realm leaves its mark on our planet, and humans become the vehicles for the arrival and departure of both. From our vantage point, heaven and hell are more present day realities than post-death destinations. To focus on the future at the expense of the present would be missing the point completely. So with this shift in perception, as Christians, we move from being escape artists to Renewal Artists.

Any thoughtful conversation about heaven and hell eventually leads to a curiosity around God's credibility and character. On a good day, God appears to be a hero, saving the day for helpless humanity. Hymn writer Fanny J. Crosby put it this way:

To God be the glory, great things He has done;
So loved He the world that He gave us His Son,
Who yielded His life an atonement for sin,
And opened the life gate that all may go in.

On a bad day, God is a backstabbing traitor. Hymn writer David Bazan adds this observation:

When you set the table
and when you chose the scale
Did you write a riddle
that you knew they would fail?
Did you make them tremble
so they would tell the tale
Did you push us when we fell?
What am I afraid of?
Whom did I betray?
In what medieval kingdom does justice work this way?
If you knew what would happen and made us just the same
then you, my Lord, can take the blame

A fair reading of the Scriptures tells the story of a God who already has and ultimately will cure humanity of its sin. (2 Timothy 1:8,9; Revelation 13:8; Philippians 1:5,6;) It's a tale of a people and planet reclaimed, restored, redeemed and reinvented. A narrative where humanity is invited, yet free to choose, whether or not to participate in the fix-it job. Everyone is in unless they opt out.

From here the big picture gains new clarity. We track with what God has done, biblical flash-forwards reveal what is to come, and in turn, we become aware of the part we were always meant to play.

We Re-Order the world when we live as Renewal Artists, working hand in hand with God for the redemption of all things.

"Hell is where sin eventually leads; it is the endpoint of the path away from God—a state of being outside the presence of God. When we see the worst of what goes on in this world, we can see that hell is not only a place people might go after death, but the condition of destruction and utter misery in which people can find themselves here and now." -Debra Rienstra

"The gospel, you see, is not just a message for individuals, telling them how to avoid God's wrath. It is a message about a kingdom, a society, a new community, a new covenant, a new family, a new nation, a new way of life, and therefore, a new culture. God calls us to build a city of God, a New Jerusalem." -John Frame

"Campaign for Real Humanity" teaching series art.

SURVIVAL OF THE WEAKEST

"Injustice is not an accident." -Gustavo Gutiérrez

Even when we suffer a small taste of injustice it is next to impossible to get the remnants out of our mouths. And after repeated violations we turtle and convince ourselves that we are justified in only looking after ourselves. Some call it a protection mechanism, others call it an excuse.

"If this is going to be a Christian nation that doesn't help the poor, either we've got to pretend that Jesus was just as selfish as we are, or we've got to acknowledge that he commanded us to love and serve the needy without condition, and admit that we just don't want to do it." -Stephen Colbert

The answer is not pity, or giving away more money, or elevating everyone to at least the middle class. The whole system is broken. Changing the oil will not repair the tail lights or cause a new muffler to grow where the old one rusted away. We don't need medicine, we need the cure.

"There is no peace because there are no peacemakers. There are no makers of peace because the making of peace is at least as costly as the making of war—at least as exigent, at least as disruptive, at least as liable to bring disgrace and prison and death in its wake." -Father Daniel Berrigan

Peace is expensive because the cost is personal. Refusing to play the game by its rules is a surefire way to lose. We need new coordinates for power, justice and vulnerability. We need to move away from servicing clients to cultivating community. The Good News for the poor [and don't be fooled—poverty comes in all shapes and smells] must migrate from the grandstands to living rooms, kitchens and backyards. The resistance begins in our homes. Food, shelter and long standing friendship. We undermine wickedness when we love people as people, and not pet projects.

"True peace is not merely the absence of tension, but the presence of justice and brotherhood."
-Martin Luther King Jr.

We Re-Order the world when we give, loan, love and linger without expecting anything in return.

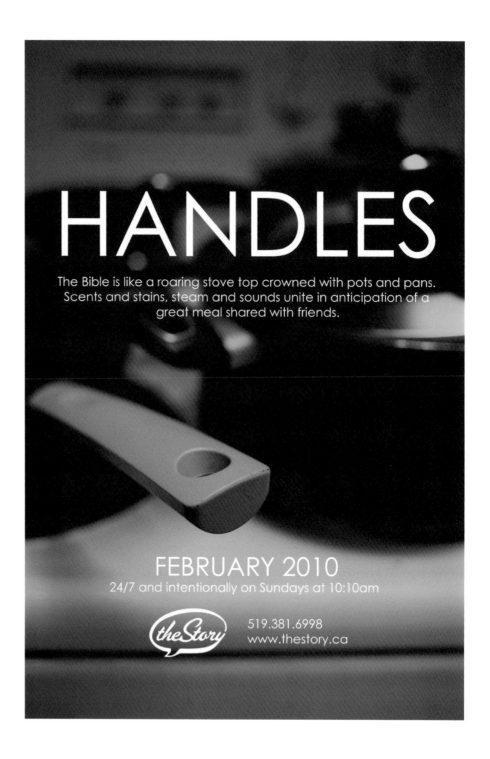

"Handles"
teaching series art.

HANDLES

"You can't help nobody if you can't tell them the right story." -Jack Cash, Walk the Line

If Scripture is a means of God's self revelation, then understanding it (on its terms and not ours) is of primary importance. Grabbing it by the right handle (literal parts as literal, figurative as figurative, historical as historical etc.) not only bring life to the reader, but also protect the text from saying, and humanity from doing, things that were never meant to be said or done.

Understanding that the Scriptures are being co-authored—that it's God's story told through human lives and means—reminds us of the intimacy shared between Creator and creation. Continually adapting the text assures the reader that it has no shelf life, that its Truth is without expiry date. When we pick it up by this handle, the Bible becomes more a transformational document then an informational one—which really has been God's ultimate point in the first place. The Bible is an experience to be entered, and not a book that one should probably read.

From whisper to print then back to whisper. Living and life giving, the Scriptures are a collection of images, a series of revealing finger prints that tell of the Divine Mystery. But this isn't the kind of mystery that is to be solved. Instead, it's a mystery that permeates all, revealing and inviting humanity into God's staggering care for the world.

Open to interpretation, but bound to community, the Bible transcends language and context to become an experience. Tragedy, comedy, fairy tale woven together from past through present and into future—it's God's epic in progress.

These stories are Handled. Handled in the sense that they've intentionally been passed down to us through human hands, for better or for worse. But also Handled in the sense that one needs to know how to pick them up in order to be fed and not burned.

In this light, it's not so much we that read the Scripture, but that the Scripture reads us. Signaling who we are, where we're from, and where we're headed, it's these whispers from the Divine Mystery that cut and heal, break and form. Something's cooking.

We Re-Order the world when we allow our story to be found in God's story.

"I always thought of my life as a story; if there is a story there must be a story teller." -G.K Chesterton

"The Bible is essentially an open, imaginative narrative of God's staggering care for the world, a narrative that feeds and nurtures us into an obedience that builds community." -Walter Bruggeman

"Good Reason to Throw a Party" installation from the Tabled.ca collection.

GODISNOWHERE

Absentee Father, or Present Help.
Dead-Beat Dad, or Strong Tower.
God Is Nowhere, or God Is Now Here.

Many people have been burned in one way or another for doubting God and God's existence. Even St. Thomas, re-dubbed Doubting Thomas, was chastised and maligned for asking the question that everyone was thinking: "Is that really you, God?" Doubt has often been associated with casting shadows when in fact, doubt more likely turns all the lights on in the house unbothered by the cost of the energy bill. If anything, doubt casts light and not shadows. Doubt is good. Doubt is healthy. Doubt is a legitimate response. Doubt forces us to ask better questions.

"The only appropriate attitude for man to have about the 'big questions' is not the arrogant certitude that is the hallmark of religion, but doubt. Doubt is humble. And that's what man needs to be, considering human history is just a litany of getting shit dead wrong!" -Bill Maher

God is not threatened by disquiet or suspicion, but God does describe himself as Jealous. "Do not worship any other god, for the LORD, whose name is Jealous, is a jealous God." (Exodus 34:14) So deep is this God invested in human affairs that God is moved to jealousy. Not the jealousy of a fearful or spoiled child, but the jealousy of a spouse who has been pushed outside and left wounded by a third party who is bent on breaking up the marriage.

God is wounded. God's love for humanity has left him defenseless. So wide is God's embrace that God opens himself up to whomever will draw near whether armed with spears or soaked in tears. Nailed in place, God is wounded by a creation that has set up detours around the scene of his death and resurrection. God is wounded, not by doubt, but by misdirected traffic.

Too often well meaning folk have become prescriptive when trying to prove all things Divine. All along, however, the true proof has been the people. When we become descriptive (God is good and I will live in such a way that exemplifies that goodness) instead of prescriptive (Do's and Don'ts with no Doubts allowed), the map changes before our eyes. The detour morphs into a thoroughfare wide enough to accommodate all travelers, and direct enough to lead us swiftly to the reconciling embrace of the Great Lover.

We Re-Order the God-debate when we become living proof—signs of the Wounded Healer, signs of the Great Lover.

"Whether your faith is that there is a God or that there is not a God, if you don't have any doubts you are either kidding yourself or asleep. Doubts are the ants in the pants of faith. They keep it awake and moving." -Frederick Buechner

OUTRO
Love God, love others, tell his story.

We begin with the end—the way all creation and all creatures were intended and will one day be.

We become the Happy Ending when we root ourselves in an unfolding story of hospitality, risk, imagination, improvisation, grace, forgiveness, redemption and rebirth, wholeness, inclusion and kinship.

God makes it possible.

The church is called to make it real.

ORIGINAL LITURGIES, PRAYERS & SPIRITUAL SONGS

(2006-2012)

ADVENT & CHRISTMAS

EXPECTING

When the teenage girl missed her period, all the world could do was wait.

Advent is the season of active waiting for Christ's arrival. We intentionally relive and remind ourselves so as to not forget. We bare ourselves to the good news of the coming arrival permitting it to re-order our lives and communities.

While there is an expectation for the culmination of prophesies and promises, at the same time there's a raw humanity to it all: A teenage girl is expecting – morning sickness, cramps, unreasonable cravings. In her belly, a fetus develops in stages. In her belly she incubates hope. As Mary and Joseph sneak into Bethlehem under the stars, God smuggles himself into humanity.

Amidst the busyness of the season, may our hearts and minds be in a place of expectancy for the one who has come to make all things new.

IT'S A BOY!

Advent is a season of expectation, a season of retuning the engines of our souls. It is a season of active waiting, an anticipation of things promised and things fulfilled. Here we find the Peace that puts the pieces back together. Disarmed, we adore as crib and cross meet, unpacking the restoration of creature and creation.

In this season we'll hold closely to the story of a teen mom and unsuspecting step-dad. We'll connect the dots labeled prophecies, dreams, apparitions, great escapes and infant massacres. Steeped in hope, we'll trace the footwork of a God taking the most radical steps possible to turn the Light back on.

Jesus came as a child – may we approach him in the same way in this season of Advent.

"Ordained before the beginning of time when the Father whispered something to the Spirit and then they both stared knowingly at the Son, who happily drew the short straw." -Alain Doseger

LION ON A LEASH

The incarnation of God's Lamb is the incarceration of Judah's Lion. Swaddling straightjacket at birth, clad in stripes at death. Our flesh to wear, our death to bear.

In voluntary submission and self-admittance, the whip and chair were of no use. Jesus, the Lion on a Leash - Glory veiled, power postponed. He was leashed that humankind be unleashed from sin. Liberated from selfishness, from injustice, from misery, from all that is oppressive. Set free from fear, from pain, from gloom, from all that is death.

Penned in a cave turned manger, the Spirit that once brooded over a formless creation was born inside of space and time. The embodiment of God. Love made flesh.

Bellies swell.
A holy shotgun wedding.
Shepherds desert their posts.
The star cuts the dark and lights the way.
Wise men dream and take the back way home.
A mass extermination.
Heaven and earth linked again.
We choose the child that chooses us.

Our Jesus, the Lion on a Leash.

GOOD FRIDAY LITURGIES

I WITNESS, GOOD FRIDAY 2008

(Curator & musician(s) off to the side as to not obstruct the view of the images & tree)

Image: Eye on Record

OPENING

Is mystery more important than knowledge? When we mix confusion with wonder, sorrow with hope, is our end goal to know all the facts and have a grasp on the situation or is there something else, something just beyond our reach, something we know, yet don't fully understand?

Today we find ourselves embroiled in a paradox of emotions – we both celebrate and mourn Christ's death. Today is about pain, suffering, sorrow, degradation and the brutality of sin.

Today we find ourselves at the foot of a tree, our eyes recording information, our brains and souls organizing this data the best it can, creatively filling in the gaps with homemade and borrowed symbols, experiences, ideas and images.

Today we leverage these things in an attempt to decipher what has happened. We need to do this in honesty, and admit that we are not able to look at the cross objectively since each of us is covered in the fingerprints of our upbringing and contexts. The risk we take is that our fears, pre-suppositions and agendas will be exposed, and at worst, or maybe best, challenged.

Today we gaze at the cross, and ask the question: What does a dying God look like? What does He look like from where you sit? What has He looked like from the vantage point of those who have come before us?

Today we're going to hopscotch through symbols and imagery of the last 2000 years. We will eaves drop on people who were working out their theology out loud through art, and hopefully today, we will be able to immerse ourselves in what is both the highlight of the Christian calendar but at the same time our darkest hour.

Scripture: Luke 23:33-46
=>BLOW OUT CHRIST CANDLE
Response: Hymn: Wonderful Cross

33 LAPS AROUND THE SUN

Eyes: Wide Open, blinking; a child's eyes
Historical Image: Christ Dead on the Cross, 11th Century (images from The Passion of Christ Through the Centuries by Richard Harries)

Historical Image Description:
In the earliest depictions of the Passion that have survived, Christ is shown alive on the cross. The reason for this and the eventual move to show Christ dead on the cross is intimately related to the theological controversies of the time. The major theological issue that concerned the Church from the fourth to the eighth centuries, in one aspect or another, was the person of Christ. The church came to assert that he is truly God and truly human, yet he remains one undivided person. If this is the case then how should Christ be depicted on the cross? If he was simply shown dead, or in the tomb, people might wonder what had happened to his divinity. So it would seem that from the fourth to the end of the seventh centuries artists tried to avoid controversial questions by not showing him dead on the cross at all. In that era, Christ was at times shown with arms outstretched, head upright and eyes open, very much alive. However, between the seventh and eighth century, it seems the church resolved its doctrinal dilemmas leaving the way open to find artistic ways to represent all aspects of Christ's nature. Thus, as in this image from the 11th century, Christ would be shown dead on the cross, indicating he was indeed fully human, experiencing death just like us.

Corporate Reading: Philippians 2:5-8
Counter Image: Roadside Monument image

Counter Image Thoughts:
What does it mean for us to see God as a human? To acknowledge that divinity fused with humanity in such a way words like frail, tired, & hungry could now be used to describe God. How do we use human language and symbol to speak of God made man, enduring 33 laps around the sun then succumbing to the fate no human can escape.

In thanks, today we erect a roadside monument, a makeshift shrine. The road is stained and marked, leaving a reminder of what happened, but at the same time it continues on, hinting at life beyond death.

Creative Response: In a journal write a prayer of thanks.
Music: I Remember by The Violet Burning; lyrics on slide

BOTH AT ONCE

Eyes: Upward in reverence and awe
Historical Image: Volto Santo (Holy Face), 11th century

Historical Image Description:
In this carving, named 'Volto Santo' or 'Holy Face' we see Christ in triumph, reigning from the tree. He is depicted in a long sleeved robe, with a distinctive knotted belt, rather than in a loin-cloth and half naked. His two feet are separated but not nailed. At the time sculpture was created, the book of Revelation played a distinct role in the spiritual life of the church. In chapter 1 of Revelation, Christ is described as a high priest 'clothed with a long robe and with a golden belt.' Here we catch a glimpse of a Christ that is not only crucified but also who intercedes for us as priest and king.

Corporate Reading: 2 Corinthians 12:9,10
Counter Image: I.O.U. image

Counter Image Thoughts:
When we come to the realization that we have nothing apart from Christ, when we finally arrive at the place of submission, where we admit that we are broken and weak, it is then, and only then that Christ can invade us, relieve us, redeem us, and strengthen us.

Creative Response: Silence & Prayer. In a moment of silence and prayer, ask God to break you. If you dare, pray that your hopes, fears, ego and self-worth be submitted to Him fully that His power would be made perfect in your weakness.

OH GOD, WHERE ARE YOU NOW?

Eyes: shifting everywhere looking around, blinking
Historical Image: Menorah by Roger Wagner, 1993

Historical Image Description:
"God where are you? Where were you?" are sentiments that some have been brave enough to verbalized, and all have fearlessly thought. This image, entitled Menorah, dares to voice the question. In the foreground are victims. They convey an impression of utter, abject grief. To the left a man, staring in horror, comforts his wife. One man hides his head and bends low, unable to look anywhere; two others cover their faces with their hands as a woman looks away while she and the man next to her hold out their arms in anger and dismay. The sense of impotence and dismay make them speechless. Beyond them hang Jesus and the two thieves. Motionless. Abandoned. In the background, 7 smokestacks, arranged to resemble the Menorah, a Jewish candlestick symbolizing the presence of God. This image begs the question, 'Oh God, where are you now?"

Corporate Reading: Psalm 22:1-11
Counter Image: Holy Toast image

Counter Image Thoughts:
Is our God a God who only makes guest appearances, randomly surfacing on slices of bread and in crazed visions? Why does he appear to be speaking loud and clear to others and not me? Why does it sometimes seem that when we need him most He's the furthest away? Can He hear me scream? Can He hear me whisper? Where did he go?

Creative Response: Listen: Oh God, Where are you Now by Suftjan Stevens (lyrics on screen)

BETWEEN THIEVES

Eyes: Scowl, Disbelief, Offended, Angry
Historical Image: The First Depiction of Christ on the Cross, 5th Century

Historical Image Description:
The death sentence of a common thief? What an embarrassment, the Son of God hanging from a tree depicted here for the first time, at some point in the fifth century. Filling out the scene we find John his disciple, Mary his mother, and a soldier with spear in hand. Also pictured, in deliberate contrast, is Judas the traitor. Judas too is hanging on a tree, thirty pieces of silver spilled out onto the ground at his feet. The branch bends, almost breaking, with his weight. Christ however, appears strong, muscular, and fully alive. This is no defeated Christ: his eyes are open and head upright, his chest pushed outwards and his arms firmly stretched.

But why were the first Christians so reluctant to show Christ crucified on the Cross? Why wait until the 5th century? One reason may be that the crucifixion was, quite simply, a form of public execution, a horrible judicial torture. To an onlooker, crucifixion conveyed not only agony, but disgrace. The cross as capital punishment was an affront, an assertion of lawlessness. With this in mind, there was little motive to display Christ on the Cross, and every social reason why this should not be done. However, in the late 4th century and during the 5th, Christians did begin to depict Christ on the cross. This clearly had something to do with the fact that the emperor Constantine abolished crucifixion as a form of public execution when he became a Christian. It was fitting, then, for Christ to be shown on the Cross, for his death would no longer be interpreted as the death of a criminal, but as the saving act of a God in whom even the Emperor now believed.

Though executed as a common thief, Christ reigns from the tree with strength and power.

Corporate Reading: Romans 12:9-21
Counter Image: Between Thieve Image

Counter Image Thoughts:
Between friends. Between a rock and a hard place. Between two worlds. Between thieves. Being caught

in the middle leaves us feeling like we belong to neither side. But what if instead of feeling trapped and out of options, we were to consider our self-awareness as marching orders? What if like Christ, we've been commissioned to bring hope to those who have none? On our shift as the church, what if evil was overpowered by good?

Creative Response: Watch Bono Video

I DOUBT IT

Eyes: up in the corners, annoyed, sloughing it off, and unresponsive, half closed eyelids, rolling eyes
Historical Image: The Incredulity of Thomas, 420

Historical Image Description:
This piece is entitled "The Incredulity of Thomas". Here Thomas is shown pointing at a wound in Christ's left side. Christ holds his left hand high displaying the spot where he was pierced by the spike. Above his head are the words 'the doors were locked' from John 20:26 referencing that no doors or even the grave could keep him captive. This scene became a standard and was reproduced countless times over subsequent centuries.

However, what's most intriguing about this particular version is the alteration inflicted by an unknown contributor. At some point in time, someone felt compelled to scratch out Thomas' face, likely vilified for asking the question that everyone was thinking: "Jesus, is it really you?"

Corporate Reading: Matthew 18:1-5
Counter Image: Doubt image

Counter Image Description:
Are there any 'faceless' amongst us? If so, wear it like a badge of honour. Never be afraid to ask the hard questions. For too long has the good new of Jesus been sequestered from healthy questions and sincere doubt from those genuinely curious about the cross. Thomas asked because he sought the truth. How can one answer if no one dares ask? From the cross Jesus calls us to come close, to come as children and find rest for our souls.

Creative Response: Hymn: Come All You Weary by Thrice

SWEET JESUS

Eyes: Tearing, crying
Historical Image: Isenheim Altarpiece, 16th Century (pg 92)

Historical Image Description:
Christians had often found it impossible to believe that the divine Son of God should be shown weak and suffering on the cross. But we must understand that the weakness and suffering of Christ on the cross is an essential element to our faith. The Son of God became fully human in all aspects sharing our suffering to the full in order that He might redeem us. Interestingly, it was not until the 14th century that Christ was depicted with a crown of thorns, instead, He was shown crowned with a halo or golden wreath symbolizing majesty and victory. In some ways, that approach may have lent itself to skipping past the brutality of his death in favour of the ultimate outcome. In this piece from the 15th century, Christ is shown in sheer agony: mouth open, eyes closed and brow furrowed, stomach drawn in to the spinal column, his flesh dreadfully marked. This portrayal of Christ expresses, in the most brutally realistic way, the conviction that God himself in Christ experiences the violence of human life, of which people in the 15th century and even now in the 21st century were and are so very conscious.

Scripture: John 15:9-14a
Counter Image: Testamints

Counter Image Thoughts:
How do you make attractive that which is not?
How do you sell emptiness, vulnerability, and non-success?
How do you talk descent when everything is about ascent?
How can you possibly market letting-go in a capitalist culture?
How do you talk about dying to a church trying to appear perfect?
How do you package spilled blood?
How can a sweet taste come from a bitter cup?

Creative Response: Read Together: For Miles by Thrice

MY PERSONAL JESUS

Eyes: closed
Historical Image: Christ on the Cross (Rembrant), 1631. (pg 101)

Historical Image Description:
In the period between 1300-1500, religious art ceased to be a purely public matter. Images were present in people's homes and went with them on their travels. Very often someone who commissioned a work of religious art would have their own image worshipping Christ incorporated in the picture. Religious manuals encouraged the supplicant to imagine that they were actually present in the scene, holding the Christ Child or suffering with the adult Christ. By the 17th century, the portrayal of Jesus alone on the cross became popular. Before this time it was common to show other people present, and often the scenes became very crowded and dramatic. Yet here we find Christ alone.

Scripture: Romans 5:6-8
Counter Image: Consumer Christ

Counter Image Description:
Did Jesus simply die so that I could live the good life? Or does His death go beyond my individual life and individual wants and needs? At times the good news of Jesus has been tampered with, leveraging the needs of one people group over another. On other occasions, the good news of Jesus has been used to promote a lifestyle or even instigate war.

Let the truth be told:
Jesus died for the rich and the poor.
Jesus died for the victim and the assailant.
Jesus died for the Canadian and the Iraqi.
Jesus died for all.
Jesus died for the sake of sinners.

On the tree, Jesus bore the weight of humanity's guilt, corruption and rebellion so that all could be redeemed.

So that all could be redeemed.

So that all could be redeemed.

Including, but not limited to, you.

Creative Response: Today, may we recognize our participation in Christ's death. Symbolically, let us write our names and on these cards then hang them on the tree representing the sins that Christ bore on our behalf.

Next, unearth a cup that represents the spilt blood of Christ, then, be seated until all have been served. We will then drink together.

ENDING THOUGHTS / I WITNESS

Eyes: Staring back

As we look at Christ pinned to the tree, He looks back at us.
As the tree bends under the weight of our sins, we realize that we carry them no more.
With the taste of death still in our mouths, we must now wait.
Go, in the uneasy peace of this Good Friday.

MIRACLE TABLE

JN 2:6-11

Reading:
What were the waiters thinking as they carried out the jugs and served the wine? Did they giggle in disbelief? Did they stop and watch in curiosity as the guests took their first swig of Jesus' home brew? Did they sneak some for themselves when no one was looking?

From jugs used to hold bath water, Jesus kicks off a clean up job like none other. Taste buds: Tantalized. Formal Conventions: Reinvented. Self-disclosure: Miraculous. Literally those in attendance that could take the familiar passage to heart: Taste and see that the Lord is good!

And for the first time in his earthly ministry, people were able to see Jesus for who he really was. At the wedding table, he laid his hand down for all to see.

Have you tasted? Can you see? Or will it take another Miracle Table to make the point?

Response: Henry Poole Video Clip

WRONG TABLE

LK19:1-10; LK15:1-2

Reading:
Forget table manners - if you're with the wrong people at the wrong tables then you're doomed. Jesus knew this.

Jesus would have agreed with the Pharisees that table fellowship is, indeed, socially binding and has religious meaning, but more and other than they imagined. The very essence of Jesus' ministry and mission can be identified in his determination to sit at the Wrong Tables. He opened up a new chapter in religious history with his attitude towards sinners, but his eating with sinners added up to more than a social misdemeanor to the Pharisees.

Sitting at the Wrong Tables inevitably cost Jesus his life.

Have you ever been accused or criticized for sitting at the Wrong Table? Hopefully so.

Response: Song – Wondrous Cross

TABLE OF POWER

MT 20:20-28

Reading:
Who knew that the seating arrangement would be so pivotal? That's a lie. We've all thought about it. Power. Authority. Being right. A superiority complex even. Figuring out who's in and who's out. Figuring out who's sitting where is just a sloppy cover-up of the real issue: Self Interest.

So often we're trying to work our way up, and all the while Jesus tells us to work our way down.

"The way of the [Christian] is not the way of upward mobility in which our world has invested so much but the way of downward mobility ending at the cross. This might sound morbid and masochistic, but for those who have heard the voice of the first love and said yes to it, the downward-moving way of Jesus is the way to the joy and the peace of God, a joy and peace that is not of this world." -Henri Nouwen

Instead of playing a spiritual version of musical chairs elbowing our way to what we think is the 'most important' seat at the Power Table, may our energies turn from being served, to serving; from making something of ourselves to making ourselves nothing; from fame to obscurity; from power to powerlessness.

Response: CONGREGATIONAL PRAYER

Father, today we pray for all who suffer and are afflicted in body or in mind
For the hungry and the homeless, the destitute and the oppressed
For the sick, the wounded, and the crippled
For those in loneliness, fear, and anguish
For those who face temptation, doubt, and despair
For the sorrowful and bereaved
For prisoners and captives, and those in mortal danger

That God in his mercy will comfort and relieve them, and grant them the knowledge of his love, and stir up in us the will and patience to minister to their needs.

UNDER THE TABLE

LK 7:36-50

Reading:
That was awkward. Funny things usually happen under tables. Things we enjoy and help us seemingly get ahead, yet we'd prefer to keep hidden. And that really goes both ways. Sometimes things that are hidden also go intentionally ignored.

Jesus, however, made a point of exposing that which was hidden or ignored. Sin is the elephant in the room, and for a while there it was only Jesus what was willing to talk about it. In this specific case, the elephant was a woman under the table washing Jesus' feet with tears and hair. Or maybe the elephant here was the Pharisees themselves, unwilling to they themselves get under the table and join in on the foot washing.

That would be problematic, as it would lump them in with the woman. Sinners the whole lot. The Pharisees here were unwilling to admit their guilt, while the woman had nothing to hide.

Admitting our sin is the first step to forgiveness. That may, however, require us to get on all fours and slip Under the Table.

Response: Old Rugged Cross

CRUMBS FROM THE TABLE

MT 15:23-28

Reading:
Even the dogs eat from their master's table. Crumbs. Leftovers. Spills. What at first sounds like a backhanded compliment from Jesus towards the Gentiles ends up really being about a clarification of his mission and an opportunity to help the helpless.

For 3 years he healed with crumbs that fell from the table. Widow's son's, Centurion's servants, demoniacs foaming from the mouth. And sometimes there were so many crumbs, they need a bunch of baskets to pick up the leftovers.

Jesus came to heal: Physical ailments, empty stomachs, emotional wounds and sick souls.
Jesus still heals: Physical ailments, empty stomachs, emotional wounds and sick souls.
If you are hungry for healing, there are still Crumbs from the Table.

Response: Silent Prayer: Healing

UPSIDE-DOWN TABLE

JN 2:13-21

Reading:
Salvation is not for sale. The church is not a factory. Love is not a product to be consumed. Faith does not require an advertising campaign. Hope is not a business.

Jesus tipped tables in the temple. Say that three times slow.

Jesus tipped tables in the temple.
Jesus tipped tables in the temple.
Jesus tipped tables in the temple.

Without hesitation, Jesus sought to set the record straight. Leaving Upside-Down tables in his wake, Jesus was making a clear statement: This is not the way it's supposed to be. You've bastardized the whole thing. Turned it into a scam, a joke. What you're doing could not be farther from the truth.

Jesus tipped tables in order to redeem Redemption.

Response: Carried to the Table

EXECUTION TABLE

LK 23:32-46

Reading:
Broken for our union, Jesus lays flat on an execution table made up of two planks of wood. Once secured to the table by both metal and sin, the table is propped up vertically.

The intention was to put Jesus on brutal display as a nationalist revolutionary. The only revolution he was after, however, was a revolution of the human heart.

"The Gospel is bad news before it is good news. It is the news that man is a sinner, that he is evil in the imagination of his heart. That is the tragedy. But it is also the news that he is loved anyway, cherished, forgiven, bleeding to be sure, but also bled for." -Fredrick Buechner

Jesus brings himself to the Execution Table.
In the company of common thieves he bleeds His last.
In His death, He invites us to join Him.

Response: Jesus Paid it All

OUR TABLE

LK 22:14-20

Reading:
Brought to the table by Jesus' invite, we give thanks for the living, dying, and rising again of Jesus. In turn, we also look forward to the second coming of Christ to finally establish his Kingdom.

Amidst this hope we remember:
*The Miracle Table
*The Wrong Table
*The Table of Power

We spend time:
*Under the Table
*Eating Crumbs from the Table

Without hesitation, we:
*Turn tables Upside Down

We join Jesus at:
*The Execution Table

As we finally realize, that this table is Our Table.
This table is ours.

Response: Eucharist + Were you There

END

We were there.
And now, we wait.

Go in the uneasy peace of this Good Friday.

CAPTURED, GOOD FRIDAY 2010

Music: Wondrous Cross

CAPTIVES

Image: Lock Jar
Read: Isaiah 61:1-3

Moments after the very beginning, we locked ourselves away. We were not fooled or tricked, no one pushed us in and slammed the door behind us, nor were we forced. By our own accord we entered the cell, locked the bars and threw the keys far beyond our own reach. In search of what we thought was freedom, we entered captivity.

Today we perpetuate this very trend. In a succession of locked doors and missing keys, we put ourselves away, distancing ourselves from help and wholeness. Another day, another lock. And as the oxygen depletes so does our desire to live. Hope and life slip away together as we realize that under our own strength there is no possibility of escape.

Enter Jesus with a ring of keys that would make a janitor jealous.

Branching out in our place, our captivity becomes his, and his freedom becomes ours.

Reflection: What is your captivity? If sin is a prison with many cells, where are you currently locked up? How much longer will your sentence be?

OWNED

Image: Money Jar
Read: Luke 18:18-30

The things we own end up owning us. We outsourced our identity and became slaves to the lowest common denominator: Fear. The closer we move towards God the stronger we feel his demand to let go of the many 'safe' structures we have built around ourselves.

Our problem is that we've too much to lose to really do anything of significance. We want to be devoted, but without the mess. Inadvertently then, we limit or contain ourselves, and it's this perceived safety that ultimately leads us into destruction.

In a counter play, Jesus used the very shackles of death to bring life. He limited himself – the first time by becoming human, the second time in death. By smuggling himself into creation and allowing himself to be held captive, he makes it possible for us to see what we are doing to ourselves. And once this epiphany hits, before we know it, we realize that the Saviour has swapped positions with us. By allowing himself to be owned by death, we are no longer owned by fear, an imaginary sense of safety, and the false self.

"All sin starts from the assumption that my false self, the self that exists only in my own egocentric desires, is the fundamental reality of life to which everything else in the universe is ordered. Thus I use up my life in the desire for pleasures and the thirst for experiences, for power, honor, knowledge, and love to cloth this false self and construct its nothingness into something objectively real. And I wind experiences around myself and cover myself with pleasures and glory like bandages in order to make myself perceptible to my self and to the world, as I were an invisible body that could only become visible when something visible covered its surface. " -Thomas Merton

Response: Read Congregational Prayer (From Common Book of Prayer)

Let us pray for those who are Owned – whether by choice or default:

For the hungry and the homeless, the destitute and the oppressed
For the sick, the wounded, and the crippled
For those in loneliness, fear, and anguish
For those who face temptation, doubt, and despair
For the sorrowful and bereaved
For prisoners and captives

That God in his mercy will comfort and relieve them, and grant them the knowledge of his love, and stir up in us the will and patience to minister to their needs.

CRUSHED

Image: Can Jar
Read: Isaiah 53:4-6

Broken for our union, Jesus hangs and bleeds. Crucifixion was designed to kill people sequentially and slowly. One by one, internal organs shut down causing both pain and disgrace.

What a sight: The slumping Jesus, straining to breath, joints under severe duress, a pierced side leaking water. And for what? A medicine for sin? No! The cure!

Imprisoned by pain, Jesus delivers healing. Amidst the violence, Jesus provides peace. Not only for sick bodies, but for sick souls. By being crushed and broken, Jesus soothes and binds. Because of who He is, we can be who we are. Taking our place yet again, the great physician assumes the illness of his patients.

"The cross says 'the pain stops here.' The way of the cross is a way of absorbing pain, not passing it on."
-Parker Palmer

Response: Sing Come All You Weary (Thrice)

EAT IT, JESUS

Image: Toilet Paper Jar
Read: Matthew 27:45-48

In Jesus' day, the poorest of slaves would earn wages by way of public toilets. [show pic]
They would sit below and behind patrons with a sea sponge on a stick, and scrub them clean after they were done. At first, they used water to clean, but soon realized that people were acquiring infections, so they then began cleansing with vinegar or sour wine as a disinfectant.

A sponge, on the end of a stick, dipped in wine vinegar.

The last taste in Jesus' mouth, the last smell in Jesus' nose was the filth of human feces.

What was harder for Jesus to choke down? The wine vinegar? The fact that earlier in the garden, the Father refused to take the cup from him? Or was it the cup itself?

In exchange for the repulsive stench and taste of sin, Jesus offers us the sweet taste of salvation:

"Taste and see that the Lord is good…" (Psalm 34:8)

"How sweet are your words to my taste, sweeter than honey to my mouth!" (Psalm 119:103)

"Make a clean sweep of malice and pretense, envy and hurtful talk. You've had a taste of God. Now, like infants at the breast, drink deep of God's pure kindness. Then you'll grow up mature and whole in God."
(1 Peter 2:1)

Another lopsided tradeoff. Freely making available to us the sweet, sweet taste of salvation, Jesus seals himself away, eating every last, dirty bite of sin in our place.

Response: Watch :36 of Shawshank Redemption clip and listen to Driving on City Sidewalks tune while silently reflecting on the taste left in Jesus' mouth. Dwell on the exchange. Be reminded of the depths Jesus plumbed to bring us to the surface. Imagine the taste and texture of sin on your lips.

FINISHED

Image: Cassette Tape Jar
Read: Sections of Psalm 22 side by side with selections of Matthew, Luke & John

Psalm 22:1
My God, my God, why have you forsaken me? Why are you so far from saving me, so far from the words of my groaning?

Matthew 27:46
About the ninth hour Jesus cried out in a loud voice, "My God, my God, why have you forsaken me?"

Psalm 22:7-8
All who see me mock me; they hurl insults, shaking their heads: He trusts in the LORD; let the LORD rescue him. Let him deliver him, since he delights in him.

Matthew 27:43-44
He trusts in God. Let God rescue him now if he wants him, for he said, 'I am the Son of God.' In the same way the robbers who were crucified with him also heaped insults on him.

Psalm 22:14
I am poured out like water, and all my bones are out of joint. My heart has turned to wax; it has melted away within me.

John 19:34
One of the soldiers pierced Jesus' side with a spear, bringing a sudden flow of blood and water.

Psalm 22:17-18
I can count all my bones; people stare and gloat over me. They divide my garments among them and cast lots for my clothing.

Luke John 19:36; 23:34
Not one of his bones will be broken...Jesus said, "Father, forgive them, for they do not know what they are doing." And they divided up his clothes by casting lots.

Psalm 22:34
They shall come and shall declare His righteousness to a people yet to be born—that it is finished!

John 19:30
Jesus said, It is finished: and he bowed his head, and offered up his spirit.

Jesus sung his way to the end. The Psalms were often sung or chanted, and here in his last mortal moments, Jesus bursts into a fan favourite. Though scripture does not record Jesus singing the entire tune, it doesn't matter. Whether he did or not, those within earshot would have instantly recognized the tones and lyrics. Perhaps they automatically began to hum along 'til they caught themselves and put two and two together. For in that moment, heritage, hope, truth and liberation intersected. In that moment, he illuminated to them that the story had already been written. In that moment he filled their hearts and heads with a new soundtrack - Replacing the song of pain and despair with the new song. A hymn of praise. A song of joy. A ballad for heavy hearts and dark nights. An anthem of deliverance - The soundtrack for life!

Response: Sing City on a Hill (Braddigan)

DEAD

Image: No Holes in the Lid Jar
Read: Luke 23:44-46; Galatians 5:1

No star hung over Bethlehem on that night. For Jesus, it was as if someone forgot to poke holes in the lid of his existence, and he finally breathed his last.

Freeing us from our death, Jesus invites us into his.

"The way of the [Christian] is not the way of upward mobility in which our world has invested so much but the way of downward mobility ending at the cross. This might sound morbid and masochistic, but for those who have heard the voice of the first love and said yes to it, the downward-moving way of Jesus is the way to the joy and the peace of God, a joy and peace that is not of this world." -Henri Nouwen

Response: Listen to Wake up Dead Man (U2)

PICNIC IN A CEMETARY

Image: Checkered Cloth Jar

Jesus' body is taken down. His disciples are scattered, but as their minds race recounting the events of the craziest day of their lives, there's one image, one memory that rises above the rest. What seemed confusing at the time, now makes sense – sort of.

Read: 1 Corinthians 11:23-26

Jesus was arranging the details of his own wake - The funeral of God, a picnic in a cemetery, a swig of wine and a pinch of bread. But this meal is more than a reminder: it's a commissioning. And it's more than just a symbol: it's the real time presence and announcement of God's kingdom that carries with it a sense of responsibility and movement.

On the cross, Jesus was broken and poured out. The picnic in a cemetery reminds us to be the same. Broken: Aware of our need for God's healing and grace.

Poured Out: Active in the liberal distribution of God's healing and grace.

With this in mind, I invite you to the picnic.

Response: Communion in a Jar (slices of bread and grape jelly)
Music: Deep were his Wounds, Red+Hallelujah (Cohen) and Old Rugged Cross

OUTRO

Once we were trapped, but now we've been freed.
Once we were captives, but now we've been liberated.

In the great exchange, Jesus took our place.
Death by love.

God came to earth, and we murdered him.

It should've been you and me who died that day.
But it wasn't.

And now, we wait.
Go in the uneasy peace of this Good Friday.

HOOKED

We know all the stories. We've heard them so many times that their details bleed into another so much so that its getting hard to tell them apart or even establish an accurate timeline. Somewhere near the beginning we chose a certain tree and its promise of god-like power. And we've heard that sometime before that, you chose another tree in an act of surrendering power. Weaved through these stories arms continue to be taken up, some twisted, and at least one set pinned back.

And so the story goes.

In the meantime, we're full of theories, but short on explanations. We're maxed out with frustration, but we've run out of fingers to point.

And even though this is a season of triumph, it feels like its too early to celebrate, and too late to do anything else.

Left with a nagging feeling, this unsettling void that leaves me with a sick question: "Who's in charge here?"

Which is it Jesus, Justice or Mercy?
Are you Exclusive or Inclusive?
Are you in this with us or are you not?
Will you just pick one for God's sakes so that we can get on with our lives?

Because we're really starting to believe that you've left us holding the burning bag of shit.

Where are you when I can't pay the rent?
Where are you when my kid remains undiagnosed?
Where are you when I'm genetically predisposed to being a drunk?

Where will you be when I put myself in compromising situations online and offline?
Where will you be when I get downsized at work?

Where have you been for China, Haiti, Libya, Winnipeg and the rest?
Justify that!

And, for the record, from this point of view your track record sucks.

You corner Abraham into nearly killing his kid?
You let Moses wander aimlessly for 40 years then never let him into your promised land?
Job loses his whole family!
John loses his head!
Israel gets steam rolled by the world's super powers time and time and time again?

Where is this table you set before us in front of our enemies?

And all this for what?
A blessing in disguise?
To teach us valuable lessons?
Torture to teach us what?
Cancer to improve us how?
Earthquakes to advance civilization in what way?

The whole bleeding, screaming, dying, lying, cheating, rotting…
This doesn't wash.

God there is no way of getting you off the hook for evil.

RESPONSE: Listen to "Did You Push Us When We Fell" by David Bazan

ON THE HOOK FOR THE ANSWERS

READ: Mark 11:27-33

"I'm not telling?" That's your answer?

You do understand that we're waiting for the big reveal, the twist, the resolve, the unveiling…you want us to enter this mystery, but we want you to solve it. Is that clear?

It feels like you're skirting the issues. Like you hadn't thought this through. We ask questions, you respond with riddles. We want answers, you want to tell stories of bread and weeds and loose change and virgins with lamps.

We feel like we have to make up excuses for you whenever evil has its way with those we hold dear. We're tired of excuses and dangling loose ends. Give us the hard facts and data we crave. Information is power… and thanks to you, we have neither.

RESPONSE: Sing "He Never Said a Mumblin' Word" by The Welcome Wagon

ON THE HOOK FOR THE TAB

READ: Mark 12:41-44

Are you kidding? You want everything from people who have nothing? This is disgraceful at best. You want the poor to keep giving even though they have nothing to begin with? What's worse is that you claim that everything we have comes from you...so really, this is nothing more than exquisite laundering scam...we borrow from you to pay you off. And the more we pay, the farther in debt we become.

Nice racket.

Then you have the audacity to claim that your salvation is free?

Well then it appears that...
"At its root, therefore, the Gospel is immoral, not moral: it lets scoundrels in free, for nothing." -R.F. Capon

You ask me for everything, yet you let me, and others in, based on nothing?

We're confused.

God there is no way of getting you off the hook for the tab.

RESPONSE: Congregational Prayer

For the hungry and the homeless, the destitute and the oppressed
For the sick, the wounded, and the crippled
For those in loneliness, fear, and anguish
For those who face temptation, doubt, and despair
For the sorrowful and bereaved
For prisoners and captives and those in mortal danger

God, have mercy
Be Comfort, for all in sorrow
Be Strength, for all who suffer
Be Peace, for the overwhelmed
Be Hope, for the hopeless

ON THE HOOK FOR PROMISES MADE

READ: John 14:1-4

We are so weary of promises. In our experience they've become disposable, nothing more than slick marketing tricks by entities that have bankruptcy protection insurance. They only take care of themselves when they promised that they would take care of us.

When you made all your promises, were your fingers crossed behind your back?

Sometimes it's hard to blame you, especially with what must be an unending stream of requests and inquiries.

Will you make good on what you promised? On all, not some or select? Sometimes we wonder if you bit off more than you could chew.

Regardless…
God there is no way of getting you off the hook for the promises you've made.

RESPONSE: Bruce Almighty Clip – 00:00-01:36

ON THE HOOK FOR ALL RERUNS, RETURNS & REBOOTS

READ: Luke 15:7; 15:9-10; 15:31-32

Sometimes we feel that our lives amount to nothing more than one long losing streak. We lose ourselves in a series of thoughts, scandals and wild goose chases. We lose our jobs, we lose our homes. We lose our kids in grocery stores, we lose our tempers, we lose hope, we lose faith.

All this losing makes us feel guilty and ashamed because we feel that we're not good enough to keep it together. Along the way, we've cheapened grace a thousand times and usually it's on purpose.

"My Lord God, I have no idea where I am going. I do not see the road ahead of me. I cannot know for certain where it will end. Nor do I really know myself, and the fact that I think I am following your will does not mean that I am actually doing so. But I believe that the desire to please you does in fact please you. And I hope I have that desire in all that I am doing. I hope that I will never do anything apart from that desire. And I know that if I do this you will lead me by the right road, though I may know nothing about it. Therefore I will trust you always though I may seem to be lost and in the shadow of death. I will not fear, for you are ever with me, and you will never leave me to face my perils alone." -Thomas Merton

We hate to admit it, but this one's on you too, Jesus.

Every time we have to reboot, every time we have to return, the rerun of loss after loss after loss…We do not have the spiritual or physical constitution to be found blameless. It's a lose/lose situation if we attempt to make a go of life on our own.

God there is no way of getting you off the hook for the reruns, returns and reboots.

RESPONSE: Silent Prayer

ON THE HOOK FOR THE DOUBTERS, DENIERS & BETRAYERS

After a while all our stories begin to carry the same rhythm and weight.

One expense too many. (Rich Young Ruler in Luke 18)
Two deaths for the price of one. (Judas in Matthew 26 & 27)
Three denials before the lone rooster crow. (Peter in Matthew 26)

On our best of days we doubt, on our worst we deny and betray. And it's you that put us in this situation.

"They hated me, they'll hate you." -Jesus
"Pick me or pick your family." -Jesus
"Unless you take up your cross and die to yourself, you're not worthy of me." -Jesus

How could we not doubt?
How could we not deny?
Can you blame us for betraying?

It's hard not to feel like this is a big set up where we become the victims…or suckers at the very least.
If this is your game and we have to play by your rules then one thing is for sure:

God there is no way of getting you off the hook for the doubters, deniers and betrayers.

RESPONSE: Sing "Wondrous Cross"

ON THE HOOK FOR THE CURE

READ: Luke 8:22-25

Do we have to wake you every time we're about to drown? Are you toying with us? Walking on water; water into wine…quit it with the cheap parlor tricks. What we need is for you to stay alert!

We are sick.
We are in pain.
We are suffering.
We are weak.
We are scared.
We can't excuse or even execute ourselves.

You say there is purpose to all of this, but we're starting to feel like this is one big accident waiting to happen. How can we share in your suffering when we can barely carry our own?

If you really made us, if you really know us, if you truly remember that we are but dust then it is you who are responsible.

God there is no way of getting you off the hook for the cure.

RESPONSE: Listen then Sing "It is Finished"

ON THE HOOK FOR EVIL

READ: John 17:1-5

Jesus reaches out and touches the leper. Somehow, instead of the infection being passed to him, his wholeness, his 'cleanness,' is transmitted to the leper instead.

Jesus allows himself to be touched by the woman with the issue of blood, whose very touch would render someone else unclean; but power flows instead from him to her, and she is healed.

He touches the corpse of the widow's son and instead of Jesus contracting uncleanness, the corpse comes back to life.

He identifies with our brokenness.
With our affliction he was afflicted.
He implicates himself and negotiates good and evil, light and dark, humanity and divinity.

The wounded healer, Jesus.

Mary of Bethany anoints him for burial; Simon of Cyrene carries the cross; Barabbas goes free; one group curses, the other repents; bystanders mock, soldiers gamble, a centurion stops for a moment in his tracks.

"What the Gospels offer is not a philosophical explanation of evil, what it is or why it's there, nor a set of suggestions for how we might adjust our lifestyles so that evil will mysteriously disappear from the world, but the story of an event in which the living God deals with it." -NT Wright

"Instead of standing at some antiseptic distance from our agonies and our failures, he comes to meet us in the very thick of them. He dies in our death, he becomes sin for our sins…[Thus] evil is where we meet God . -R.F. Capon

The great physician infects himself with the poison to become the cure. The universe's first vaccine becomes the remedy for all evil. Evil is taken out as it is taken in.

RESPONSE: Sing "What Can Wash Away Our Sin?"

ON THE HOOK FOR ME

Jesus hung on the tree of death so that I could have the tree of life.

Jesus was literally on the hook for evil, putting the 'Very' back in God's 'Good' creation.

Yes, he is literally on the hook for evil.
He is literally on the hook for you, for me.

We are awakened to this as we move from blame to realization.
Of course Jesus is on the hook.

Jesus is literally on the hook for the Answers
Jesus is literally on the hook for the Tab
Jesus is literally on the hook for the Promises Made
Jesus is literally on the hook for the Reruns, Returns & Reboots
Jesus is literally on the hook for the Doubters, Deniers & Betrayers
Jesus is literally on the hook for the Cure
Jesus is literally on the hook for Evil

He assumes responsibility for good gone bad, for perverted freedom, for calculated injustice, for bridges burned and walls put up.

For the kid that has no chance and the parent that put them in that fix
For the abused and forgotten
For the rich and the poor
For hungry and the obese

Jesus is squarely on the hook so we don't have to be
Jesus is literally on the hook for Me
Jesus is literally on the hook for You

I need this meal
We need this meal

READ: 1 Corinthians 11:24-26

What you must solemnly realize is that every time you eat this bread and every time you drink this cup, you reenact in your words and actions the death of the Master. You will be drawn back to this meal again and again until the Master returns.

RESPONSE: Communion
*Participants write name?/the heavy?/categories? with sharpie on stone. Stones hung on Hook Tree; take elements

OUTRO

In our place, Jesus is on the hook for all things evil.

And now, we wait.

Go in the uneasy peace of this Good Friday.

PRAYERS

By Nathan Colquhoun

SUBMISSION AS SUBVERSION

May we be the kind of community where
Wives love their husbands and
Husbands love their wives
and where
Husbands and Wives mutually sacrifice and submit to one another

May we be the kind of community where
Parents listen to their children
Children obey their parents
and where
Children and Parents seek understanding and not manipulation or control

May we be the kind of community where
Others become important to us
Our Lives don't oppress any other
and where
We seek justice and peace rather than excess and luxury

May we be the kind of community where
Children are given opportunity to dream
Children are given freedom to be different
and where
We create environments for selflessness instead of selfishness

May we be the kind of community where
Those we don't understand are welcomed
Those we don't see are sought
and where
We consciously create an alternatives where there seems to be none

Amen

WAITING WELL

God, Let us wait well
While we wait, we will restore with you
While we wait, we will redeem with you
While we wait, we are transformed by you

Jesus, Let us wait well
While we wait, we hope for your presence
While we wait, we pray for peace in tension
While we wait, we hope for change around and in us

God, Let us wait well
While we wait, let us remember your promise
While we wait, let us remember those who have waited before
While we wait, let us remember you wait with us

Jesus, Let us wait well
While we wait, may we beat swords into plowshares
While we wait, may we love where there is hate
While we wait, may we live as if the wait is over

Amen

LET US NOT REWRITE HISTORY

God, forgive us for our formulas
Forgive us for thinking we know how it works
Forgive us for thinking we can see clearly
Have mercy on us, as our understanding is small

We are blind
We are unable to see everything you are doing
We are unaware of how you are at work
We are unsatisfied with not knowing

So give us eyes to see
Give us ears to hear

Show me where you have given grace
So I may extend the same grace to others

Show me who my neighbours are
Show me where you are at work
Break my formulas
Show me grace instead

Amen

BEING CAUGHT

God thank-you for sending your son to take our place
We know we are sinful and aren't able to stand up to your standards
We accept your grace
Help us learn to live in it
Help us not hoard it

Thank-you for loving us because of who we are and not what we do
We know we can't really live the lives we were meant to
We receive your grace
Teach us to live in it
Teach us to share it

Thank-you for the strength to do what is right
We know we wouldn't without it
We receive your strength
Remind us that it is yours
Remind us that it's for others

Thank-you for your inclusive good news
We know that all have been offered acceptance
We receive your acceptance
Remind us why
Remind us that its for all

Amen

DEBT

God, thank-you for your blessings
Thank-you for our wealth
Thank-you for our community

Let us not turn your blessings into curses
Let us not hoard your wealth as if it's ours
Let us not focus on ourselves but each other

God, thank-you for this story
Thank-you for the barns we already have
Thank-you for our full stomachs

Let us tell this story with humility
Let us not be afraid of empty barns
Turn our ears to empty stomachs and hearts

God, thank-you for your story
Thank-you for grace when we fail
Thank-you for your promise of abundance

Let us not turn your story into selfishness
Allow our failure to highlight your grace
May we build different kinds of barns
May we throw different kinds of parties

God, even though we are poor
Let us make many rich
Even though we are sorrowful
Let us always rejoice
Even though we have nothing
May we possess everything.

Amen

CRUNCHING NUMBERS

God, we know that we don't have what it takes
We know that we are fallen, sinful people
We know that even in our best moments we fail to meet your demands

So teach us more about your grace
Remind us again of what is at stake
Take our lives and accept our death

It is in the very act of dying that your grace abounds
Yet we can't seem to bring ourselves to do it
So take our inability as our death

We know your way is good
Give us strength to die daily
Give us hope to see the eternal
Give us death so we can have true life

Amen

THE MUSTARD SEED

Remind us of our smallness
Remind us that you are still working, even when we can't see
Remind us that your kingdom exists all around us
Remind us that hope is found buried and covered in dirt

Transform our desires away from the big and loud
Point them to the small and insignificant
Remove our pride to become known and important
Point them to being unknown and servants

We trust and hope that your kingdom will reign
But not through our sinful pursuits or shortcuts
We trust that you will grow your own kingdom
And we will wait patiently

Amen

YEAR END PRAYER 2010

We come here together for lots of different reasons
Some because this is the only thing that makes sense
Some because its where we feel loved
Some because we want to learn more
May you use our reason and intellect

We've all grasped at different handles
Some have grabbed too many
Some haven't grabbed enough
Some refuse to grab anything
May you use our flawed logic

We all come from different ways of thinking
Some think everyone else is wrong
Some think they never could be right
Some think they have lots to learn
May you use our stubbornness and humility

We are drawn by the mystery of God coming to earth
We long to be part of the revolution
We long to share the good news
We long to bring justice
May you give us strength to complete the race

We can't make sense of everyone's story
We rewrite people's history
We make up formulas
We give answers where there are none
May you give us peace and love through mystery and paradox

We give you our hearts and our heads
Our hands are the hardest to give to you
Our thoughts and feelings only have meaning through action
Our default is to do what comes easiest
May you give wisdom that we may learn discipline

We live in an unfinished state

Our heads talk us in and out of the good news
Our hearts nudge us to be more complete
Our hands drag along behind us trying to keep up
May you remind us that you've already completed the work for us

May we bring everyone to our table, as we sit at your table
May we risk by having nothing, so that we may have everything
May you root us in your story, this community and the world's good news

Amen

CREATION

God of heaven and earth. God who sees us. God who hears our cry.

We thank-you for creating us and creating this world.
We know you are not done, and that this world is far from the good that you intended.
Thank-you for being a God who does not give up and who pursues his purposes till completion.
We are hard up now because it feels at times like you are not around, like creation is getting worse.
Sometimes it feels like we are getting worse and less in tune with you.

Give us comfort and peace in knowing that one day you will redeem all of creation.
Give us comfort and peace in knowing that one day these problems will disappear.
Give us comfort and peace in knowing that you care more than we do and are passionately pursuing your purpose in us and throughout all your creation.

May we be your creation, and may you look at our lives and say it is good.
May we be good to your creation, and good to each other
May we long for the image of God in our lives in everything we do.

God of heaven and earth. God who sees us. God who hears our cry.

Teach us to create and redeem along side of you.
Teach us to see your creation behind everything, good and bad

God of heaven and earth. God who sees us. God who hears our cry.
Have mercy on us.

Amen

WHEN BELIEFS DON'T EQUAL ACTION

Lord forgive us, for we are hypocrites
We believe one thing and do another
We say one thing and never back it up
Our lives are a mess
One contradiction after another

We believe that you died
We believe that you rose
We believe that you will save us
We believe that you reign
We don't live like you did any of those things
We don't live like you are doing anything now

We believe we should care for the earth
But we destroy it as soon as we wake up

We believe that we should care for each other
But we hurt each other all day long

We believe that we should be selfless
But we are selfish

We believe that we should help the poor
But we only help ourselves

Our faith is dead
Because our deeds are dead

So God we sit humbly at your feet
Recognizing our inability to live out our beliefs
We have faith that you are transforming us
We have faith that you have made a way
We enter into your story and let you do the transforming
We place everything before you as an offering
We don't just want to change what we believe
We want to change how we see

Amen

IMAGING A NEW ECONOMY

God forgive us for not truly living in your kingdom.
Whether it be through our money, time and relationships
We always tend to make it about us
We never think twice
Before following blindly what we think is normal

God forgive us for being addicted to our cash-flow
For feeling secure when we have money in the bank
For feeling valuable when we buy new things
For feeling powerful when we show off

God forgive us for living by our own rules
For living by our own values
For dictating what we think we deserve
For trying to control outcomes

Free us to live the way you created us to be
Free us to live generously
Remind us of our insurmountable value
Remind us that love doesn't come through things

Give us dreams that start with you
Give us dreams that aren't selfish
Give us dreams that help the world
Give us boldness to live backwards to this world
Give us boldness to live without idols
Give us boldness to proclaim with our lives
The kind of life that you made possible

Amen

EASTER SUNDAY MORNING

It was a long three days
It came as a surprise
We went back to fishing, back to our normal lives
We didn't wait, we gave up

But you didn't give up
You came to us instead
You came to us while we were still fishing
Still sinning

We really didn't think this was going to happen
But now that it did
Now that you are standing here in front of us
The holes in your hand, the look on Mary's face
It's starting to make sense

You died so we didn't have to
We die, so we don't have to
You hung on that cross, in such a shameful way
So broken, so distraught that God forsake you
We felt forsaken too
We believe, help us in our unbelief

You lived the life that Israel couldn't
You died the death that Israel wouldn't
All these prophets words started to come back to us
You were the suffering servant
You were the broken Saviour
This is what we've been waiting for

This is Abraham's promise being fulfilled
Jacob, Isaac, Joseph, David…
You were the light to the nations, you blessed the nations
You freed Israel from the law
You freed us from it as well

We welcome your death
Because this morning, even death doesn't stay
Teach us how to die
So that we may live
Teach us how to live
So that we may die

We accept your gift
Your sacrifice
Your presence
Thank-you

Thank-you for everything
Creation
Your Patience
Your Direction
Your Way
Your Death
Your Grace

We rejoice in your resurrection
We accept your new way of life
Give us strength to keep on this new life
You've turned back news into good news
Now we will turn this good news into real life

You have risen
We choose to follow you
Be here with us

Amen

REMEMBERING WHO WE ARE

May you remember who you are
We are citizens of God's Kingdom
We are God's children
We are disciples of Christ

May you remember what your task is
Our task is to model citizenship in God's Kingdom
Our task is to love one another and bear each other's burdens
Our task is to give and serve each other and the world

May you remember God's grace and all He's done
We confess our memory is weak
We confess we are prone to leave you
We confess this is difficult and we don't always care

May you remember this is a story of freedom and liberation
We will be a community of compassion
We will be a community of forgiveness
We will be a community of confession
We will be a community of love and peace

Amen

LOVING THE OTHER

Merciful God,
We need a new perspective
We need to accept that our perspective might be wrong
We need the courage to see live through the eyes and ears of the other

Compassionate Father,
Give us love for those who aren't like us
Remove our hands from our ears and silent our voices
Take the stone out of our hands

Loving Saviour,
We repent for the times we did the wrong thing

We repent for the times when we did nothing
We repent for the times we don't care

Righteous Judge,
Give the angels in our midst courage and strength
Let us not kill, ignore or disregard them
Give us willingness to live like angels

Amen

THE STORY OF SALVATION

The revolution confronts us every day
Do we want to join in?
Will we live as if Jesus is alive and well today?
Or will we sit back take in the sights?
Will we hope that believing it happened is good enough?

God has been orchestrating a story
It is so grand that it doesn't leave anyone out
When things seem to go in a bad direction
God uses it to show he expected it all along
In God's story, death is actually life, empty is actually full
What feels like chaos is actually order

What God has promised has moved forward to meet us.
What we need, stares us in the face
From this point forward, we are getting back on track
We will finish God's story out faithfully and not selfishly

May we remember that salvation has already happened.
May we live like salvation is real
May we respond well to the news before us
May we know your rescuing power.

Amen

SONGS

HOLY GHOST
By Darryl Silvestri

where is
the
fairness
in all of your absented charity
this colloquial silence, just spare me
with one set of footprints,
don't you carry me?

you bend
the
rules and
my life hangs in the balances
twisted games of snakes and ladders and
(for all intents and purposes)

i would
if
i could
recant all my past endorsements
accumulated and cast before your
impotent omnipotence

mighty to save all but the innocent
a deft will catered to the invalid

i went out
to search for an angel in a cloud
all i found
was a ghost and it haunts me now

WHEAT AND WEEDS
By Darryl Silvestri

giver of breath
what waste in generosity
swollen breast
retreated ebb
equal pay for truth and travesty
to what end
do you intend
this impartial battery?

justice,
have i alluded thee?
karma's tit for tat, is juvenile
but controllable at least
but this
i am tares and
i am wheat
i am triumph and defeat
and my capillaries have
never been in need
all i can do
is receive

you have yet
to acquiesce
grace knows better
than to bate its breath

WHEN THE SEARCH PARTY BECAME A MAN HUNT

By Darryl Silvestri

we caught a glimpse of the red constrast
in the grove
possessed with the incessant desire
to hold and to behold
we fought through the fog in the dark
but we were lost
this is the hunt for the divine fox

and i know in the end it could only lead to ruin

we load our guns
to search for you
you fill our lungs
to hunt for you

and the hunt weathers heavy on
the soul
what a waste to wholly embrace the pursuit
of control
were we not made to dominate and subdue
and our praise, just one of the ways
we hope enslaves you

to foil our plans
you placed yourself into our hands

my deliverer is coming
my deliverer is standing by

we war against
you and all your dreams
you carry us
through the emptiness of autonomy

THANKYOUS

The bibliography will name names.

In no particular order, give or take, these people are the 2012 version of theStory:

Mark, Kristine, Tristan, Julia, Samantha and Jake: For filling 2 couches, making the old girl sparkle and for caring so deeply about it all.

Bruce and Natalie: For encouraging us to love and serve abroad, and for spectacular catches in center field.

Dan, Mel, Charlie and Ruby: For opening our minds and hearts a little wider.

Scott: For showing us that not all Leaf fans are crazy.

Tom and Sam: For the banjitar and for reminding us that we are worthy and loved.

Chris and Emily: For serving well and for giving it all a chance.

Mike and Shekanah: For that great quote and for the hot coffee.

Nathaniel: For the brutal honesty and generosity.

Fred and Renate: For the old-school wisdom and musical gifts.

Honie, Isaac and David: For reminding us of the Spirit's transformative work.

Robb, Melissa, Jake, Isaac, Ethan and Madison: For giving freely, serving fully, and for the pool parties.

Laura and Theo: For the piano and the love for Cuba.

Darryl and Laura: For helping at the start and crossing your fingers in hopes of returning.

Aaron, Lydia, Noah & Anna: For teaching us new things from past times and for living at the Spirit's pace.

Ian, Michelle, Gavin and Nathan: For giving your best and for the fine espresso.

Kevin, Jade, Cam and Emma: For not being afraid to ask the hard questions.

Nathan and Rachel: For being the best co-conspirator and best party planner ever.

Nathan, Carrie, Chase and Evan: For leading well and setting the standard for faithfulness.

Barry, Natalie, Talia, Avery and Parker: For giving over and above and for the gift of keeping time.

Troy, Dana, Porter and Lake: For coming home.

Geoff and Liz: For giving all of this a chance.

JJ: For the nasi gori.

Jo: For fighting the good fight.

Sarah, Ethan and Ella: For permission to hijack and sabotage everything for the cause.

John, Nora, Calvin, Shaelynn, Alyssa: For being one of the first families and for seeing this through.

Josh, Taryn, Brodie and Owen: For the willingness to be uncomfortable.

Tim: For your rockstar work with the Jr. High's and for the accordion solos.

Ron & Meagan: For your over the top generosity and for giving Sarnia a chance.

Steve, Louisa, Maya, Charlize and Aria: For being a backbone family and for being sensitive to the Spirit's leading.

Daniel: For being our minstrel, for the longest sermon in Story history (1.2hrs).

Chad and Steph: For lending a hand and a heart whenever needed.

Marty and Daneka: For the 2nd, 3rd and 4th chance on faith.

John P: For your unpredictable weekday visits.

Doug and Lynn: For taking bullets on our behalf.

Ryan, Erica and Max: For joining the family and for taking good care of the little ones.

Aaron and Danielle: For the timely encouragement and for making Sarnia home.

Mike and Katie: For the little signs on the home baked goods, and the brilliant, show-stopping saves on Monday nights.

Nathaniel & Julie: For being courageous.

And then there are those whose influence is felt even though we don't always get to be with them:

Fitch: For the counsel and desperately needed encouragement.

Siebert: For footing the bill and giving us a chance.

Capon: For the master class in writing and theology.

Doseger: For showing us what the Good News looks like in real life.

The 1975 Philadelphia Flyers: For showing us it can be done.

WestWinds in Jackson: For setting the target for excellence.

Daniel and Domenica: For loving kids that you don't even know.

Ken and Val: For showing how hammers and nails, meals and calls are means of the Kingdom.

Fiorenza: For never screening calls.

Duncan: For trading stories.

Vatche: For the sign and door decal.

Blondel: For listening.

Rude: For the icons.

Melles: For never mincing words.

Peterson: For being present.

Plintz: For remembering when others forgot.

The Story Party Game night
All Ages   07, 2010 November.

7pm

Bring sndks

bring your vidio games

shake
it